Maritime Traditions of Medieval Malabar

Dr. V. Kunhali

Indian Council of Historical Research
35, Ferozeshah Road, New Delhi

in association with

ANAMIKA PUBLISHERS & DISTRIBUTORS (P) LTD.
4697/3, 21A, Ansari Road, Daryaganj, New Delhi 110 002
Phones: 011-2328 1655, 011-43708938
E-mail: anamikapublishers@yahoo.co.in

First Published 2020

ISBN 978-81-7975-842-7

PRINTED IN INDIA

Published by Anamika Publishers & Distributors (P) Ltd., 4697/3, 21A, Ansari Road, Daryaganj, New Delhi 110002. Typeset by Shivani Computers, Delhi 110093 and Printed at Vikas Computer & Printers, Tronica City, Ghaziabad

Contents

Glossary

Alim	:	Religious scholar
Aliyyul Kufi	:	Sheikh Aliyuul Kufi, who settled in Peringathur village in 16th century
Amana	:	A trusted property or vow made in the name of God
Aniyam	:	Front portion of a ship
Anjuman	:	The trade organization that takes the origin of the word from Hanjamana or Anjuwannam
Asad	:	Sher, Lion
Athani	:	Granite, Laterite or wooden structures constructed as charity on way sides for head load carriers.
Al-Qaseer	:	A luxury ship recently built in Beypore
Bavar	:	The wheel, main equipment of Khalasis
Calicut Grandhavari	:	The palm leaf manuscripts in the Zamorin's Palace of Calicut.
Chopra	:	Embalming
Dargha	:	Burial place of holymen/A pilgvimage center
Dhows	:	Big ships built in Beypore
Dhikrand Dua	:	Enchanting the sacred books and Prayer.

Fanus	:	Old Kerosene lamp carried in a glass case
Gumti	:	Chief of Khalasis
Hanafi Seet	:	One of the four sects of Islamic Society
Iblis	:	Satan, Devil
Ihram	:	The first act of preparation for Haj
Ilaravu	:	Younger nights, the First fourteen nights of lunar month
Jasad	:	Body/ Lust
Kalpathu	:	Filling the gaps between the planks of a ship thrusting cotton wicks dipped in oil.
Kammalis	:	Unskilled Manual Labourers
Kannu Thurakkal	:	Opening the eye. Marking two eyes for the ship. The last rite of ship-building.
Karama	:	Supernatural powers attributed to Sufis and Divines
Karimi	:	A trade guild under which the Egyptian traders operated in Medieval times.
Karim Kallu	:	Granite in Malayalam- The Sumerian word too is Karim Kallu for Granite
Kazerunis	:	The sufi order originated from Sheikh Kazeruni of Persia. Patron Saint of Mariners.
Khalasis	:	The people launching the ship, and also the salvage team nowadays.
Khanqah	:	The head quarters or hermitage of sufi orders.
Komb	:	Branch (Mal) Here the Mast poles of the ship.
Korwan	:	The Arch Shaped Space on the rear portion of Keel to fit fan of the Engine.
Kudiyan Sangam	:	Farmers' Organization (of early 20th Century)
Liqah	:	Meeting of the Lord on the Final Day as Muslims believe.
Mestri	:	Head of Odayis/Chief of any work group.
Malabaris	:	People of Malabar. In the context of 16th century the Portuguese used the word for Kunhali Markkars and his fighters.
Mappila	:	Muslims of Malabar

Marakkar	:	Owner of a Maram or Boat
Maram	:	Timber/tree/ship
Muallim	:	Religious instructor
Meeqat	:	The places where a pilgrim for Haji Starts Haj ceremonies.
Mimber	:	Pulpit for Friday sermons.
Mulla	:	A religious functionary
Mundu	:	A cloth/bath towel
Musliar	:	The man leads prayer/gives counseling
Muthatharrib	:	The man who announces the departure of a ship in the streets.
Muwalladun	:	The progenies of Arab fathers and native women (in trade centres)
Nali	:	One measure (of cereals) equal to 1/5 of a litre.
Nakhuda	:	Captain/Lord of the Ship.
Nanth	:	The rope used by K.halasis in Bavar
Nilapaduthara	:	The raised platform were the Zamorin Rajas supervised the Mamankam festival
Odayis	:	Builders of Odam, Ship
Oteupalaka	:	Close plank'. Close to the keel.
Panam	:	A quarter rupee
Para	:	A measure (for cereals) equal to 10 litres
Qabar	:	Burial of Muslims
Qahwa	:	Spiced Coffee Arabs use
Qalandar	:	A group of faquirs pledged to perpetual wandering with little regard for life
Raeesul Muslimin	:	Head of Muslim community
Sabantra Koay (of Calicut)	:	Shah BandarKwaja, Port officer in Medieval times
Saiyu	:	Runni ng, one of the rites of Hajj
Sayyid	:	A man belonging to Prophet Mohammed's family class
Shafi Sect	:	One of the four sects of Islam.
Shart	:	Condition (for religious rites)
Sur	:	A ship constructed in Beypore on the models

		found in the port of Sur in gulf.
Thathruba	:	Announcement of departure of a ship.
Thawaf	:	Circumambulation of the shrine ofKaaba.
Therappam	:	Hundreds of logs tied together to float down the river to centres of Timber trade and mills.
Changadam	:	Same as Therapam- Also special types smaller ships used in ferries for men and Vehicles.
Uru	:	All big plank built ships constructed in Beypore
Vari	:	Rib-also frame of ship
Vavar	:	The Muslim Diety in Sabarimala, A friend of the chief Sri Ayyappan.
Warknife	:	The knife Muslims carried in old days dreaded by Britishers and confiscated.
Zakath	:	Poor right in Islam.

Foreword

This is carefully prepared and comprehensive study of Maritime Traditions of Medieval Malabar. It is also enriched by a glossary which explains the technical terms. The Medieval technology of ship-building practices in the natural harbours of Malabar is discussed in detail.

Arab geographer's accounts suggest that there existed in Arab-Persian countries, communities of ship-builders from early medieval centuries. The migrant Odayis of Malabar in the Gulf regions have transplanted and kept alive our ship-building traditions.

Since 16th century when Europeans tookover Eastern trade, we get detailed descriptions of ship building in the writings of Varthema, Barbosa and others. They studied indigenous ship-building materials, technology and construction methods.

The best timber universally acclaimed for ship-building was Teak. The construction cost was half of the European cost. Barbosa got four ships constructed in Calicut and sold them to the Merchants of Gujarat and Coramandal coast. The Dutch who followed the Portuguese in Maritime trade had to face stiff resistance in Malabar. It was this hostility that compelled the Zamurin to revive the Marakkar tradition in 1667 as evident in Calicut Grandhavari. The British who occupied Malabar in 1799 exploited the indigenous expertise. They started a Teak plantation in Nilambur, the upper basins of the Chaliyar river in 1845, to make sufficient quantity of Teak available for railways and for Dockyards of Bombay and Bassein. The British also promulgated a series of Malabar Preservation of Private Forest Acts (MPPF) to restrict cutting of certain varities of timber.

British ship-building in India progressed so well that it rivalled ship-building anywhere in the world. To compensate the loss of British ship-building yards a law was enacted that 80 per cent of the commodities imported to Britain should be brought in British built ships.

A Teak-Oak controversy developed in ship-building. When Canon balls hist Oak built ships that splinter away, while in the Teak built ships it only created a hole which could be easily repaired. It is believed that in the Battle of Trafalgar Admiral Nelson had eak built ships under his command.

The ship-building tradition of Malabar had continuous history while other centres experienced rise and fall of trade and political power.

The Author has listed 24 groups of people associated with ship building right from the tribals who help constructing timber tracks in the interior forest to the capital investors often from abroad. The expertise of Beypore Odayis to construct all types of vessals is explained, be it the 3000 year old Sumerian sewn plank ships built for Capt. Akkira Iwatta or the model of Vasco da Gama's ships.

The economy of Malabar was market-oriented under a barter system where ships had a key role. Maitime activities had so well influenced the society that even Sufi poems has Maritime similies and some of the Hindu folk Gods had headgears resembling sails. Little was written in Malayalam as the tradition was handed down to generations.

Kunjali Marakkars form an important legacy of Mariners of Malabar. Leaders of Marakkar community were conferred the Naval Captainship of the Xamorins of Calicut who fought the Portuguese from 1521 to 1599, saving Kerala culture and Malayalam language from a doom similar to Goa. The investiture of the head of the community as his Naval Captain by the Zamorins in 1667 to meet the

Dutch depredations in Malabar once again highlights the role of the Marakkar's in the history of Malabar. They organized their fighters as a Sufi brotherhood solemnized to fight unto death.

The life on board of a ship is well explained. A pious and holy air was maintained. In the European ships priests were employed by the king. Masses and confessions were held. Holywater was kept. Women were not allowed on board.

Condition of a God fearing heart is like that of sailer in a sinking ship. So people observed prayers, rituals and listend to pious sermons of holy men and sufis. Khanqahs all over the Medieval world served as ' Pious Night Clubs'. The Kazeruni Sufis were regarded as Patron Saints of Mariners in Eastern Seas.

The work is the result of painstaking studies and field works. It is also a brief sketch of social life of Malabar in Medieval times.

M.G.S. Narayanan

Acknowledgement

This work, Maritime Traditions of Medieval Malabar is a Historical, Sociological and Religious study of the Maritime people of Malabar. For a long time, I had in mind a more comprehensive work and still have a conviction that more and more information can be added to it. But the absence of sources compels me to rely almost completely on field work.

A long line of well wishers, scholars, friends and owners of ship-building yards, aged people who for fifty or sixty years worked as mariners, wood cutters, therappam workers and Odayis were my chief source of information as traditional systems remain without change.

The Indian Council of Historical Research deserves my foremost thanks for funding this research project. Thanks are due to my former colleagues Prof. M.G.S. Narayanan, Dr. M.R. Raghava Varier, Dr. E.K.G. Nambiar and my close friend (late) Prof. S.M. Mohammend Koya.

Owners of ship-building yards of Beypore, K.V. Kunhammed Koya, Mr. Mammadu Barami of Barami Ship building Company, Mr. Majeed and son Gafoor of Binafa Enterprise, deserves my heartfelt thanks. I also thank the authorities of old Areacode Juma Masjid where I copied the wall painting of the ship (Human life), an 18th century painting.

Workers of many stages, from wood cutters to the ship launching khalasis and crew who had worked on board many vessels had been kind enough to answer my quarries, deserve my thanks.

My old friend Mr. Abbobacker of Lacadcives was kind enough to let me make use of his family's mariners book, wherein every member added his own experience to be handed down to generations, deserve special thanks.

Dr. Tariq Ahamed, Chairman, Centre of Advanced Study, Department of History, AMU Aligarh, had offered all assistance for working in the centre's library and I sincerely thank my classmate.

I take the opportunity to express my deep felt gratitude to my teacher Prof. A.J. Qaisar, who initiated me to Maritime studies. Dr. Iqbal Hasnain, former Vice-Chancellor of University of Calicut had been kind enough to take me into the society for preserving the Sumerian Ship, enabling a closer study of Sewn Plank boats, deserve my heartfelt thanks.

I also thank Mr. Raman of Infratec Computers, who did all the typing and editing of the photographs for this work.

Dr. Kunhali V.

Introduction

Information gathered in many years during the course of my studies was the provocation to select this topic for research project. The paucity of reference materials was a hurdle immediately felt. Fortunately, close contact with people involved in various stages of ship-building made the task easy. For example, close relation with the chief timber merchant of Nilambur who supplied timber to ship-building yards from 1970s to 2005 was helpful in contacting 'coop' workers, Therappam Rawers and Building yard owners including khalasis of Beypore.

A good friend from Laccadives presented me his family's 'Logbook' kept as a sacred possession wherein every member added his own experience. An important fact gathered about the Laccadive people was that in Madrasa itself, students begin to study the poems by heart to fix the position of ships in relation to the position of stars.

The sailors on rivers and seas had their own pattern of behaviour, their own proverbs and jokes. Pona Thonildcu Uppu Vekkuka (load salt in the returning canoe) means conveniently make use of the returning boat. The implication is to get a work done without much labour and cost. A lot derives from this proverb.

Firstly, salt is very cheap and at the same time heavy, requiring more cargo space. It would fetch lesser profit. But every grocer's shop should have salt, and transporting salt along river to interior markets was the only possibility. If the load is sent on a returning canoe it brings profit.

Secondly, it indicates that transportation of provisions to the interior was only through rivers. Since there was hectic movement of rafts on the rivers, temporary hotels, riverine settlements and mosques sprang up.

Thirdly: It points to the absence of good roads and conveyance system.

Fourthly, it denotes some one taking advantage of other's labour. Many such proverbs, I decided not to explain.

Another word commonly used, becomes a puzzle when studied deeper. The word is 'Musliar' used in Malabar for Moulavis. The origin of the word has become subject to many disputes and debates arriving at no conclusion among Moulavis and Mullas. The Persian-English Dictionary of F. Steingass has one who gives (advices) peace. There was the custom of shipowners or captains carrying pious and holy men on board for various reasons, discussed in detail in chapter on working groups, Life Onboard and rituals.

1. To give religious instruction for passengers on leisurely hours.
2. To act as a middleman in disputes that may arise between the mariners and natives of the port they visit.
3. The most important reason is to give peace and consolace to passengers in the wake of a soul-harrowing disasters.

This third duty earned its functionary Musliar who advices people, teaches in Madrasas and lead prayers. This is another instance of a maritime functionary turning to a religious functionary in the community. Such inferences also provided inspiration to take up this study.

Ancient history of Mariners of Malabar could be gleaned from Roman contacts, where in the port of Kodungallur, Roman Ships were seen like giant horses holding heads high:

> The information of Sumerian contact and sewn plank boats are interesting. The Arabic works following Roman period are useful

> for early medieval centuries. Abulfida's note on Chaliyam (on the opposite side of Beypore) that the 'Majority of the Population is Jews' lead us to history of the beginning of Christian era. As Arab traders specially noted pepper as spices, but provides the important information of 'saj' (teak) being exported as one important item from Malabar. This teak 'The best timber in the world for ship-building' might have been used for other purposes, but mainly for ship-building. Arab geographers also tell us that "workers with their tools go to the country of coconut and get the ships constructed".

This would probably suggest an expert ship-building community existed in the Arab-Persian gulf countries also during 10-14 century. Nowadays we learn the migrant Odayis (Ship-builders) of Malabar in the gulf region. But for the early middle ages, we have no sufficient proof to establish the migration of Odayis which is quite possible in between of East-West trade, where the demand for ships were probably met with timber imported from Malabar and African coast as at least some of the historians believe.

Since 16th century, when Europeans took over eastern trade, we get detailed description of ship-building in Ludovieo Varthema and Durate Barbosa and subsequent writings. Ambitious of better profits, they studied indigenous ship-building materials, technology and construction cost. They came across the best timber, teak and for their enthusiasm, on a comparatively lesser, almost half the cost. A comparison of technology is also seen. Barbosa got four ships constructed in Calicut and sold to merchants from Gujarat and Coromandal. The cost of construction in Lisbon and Calicut was 2:1. We do not get further details in this regard. Strangely enough, one of the four ships in Vasco de Gama's convoy was named Nao, while Nao is the Indian name for ship.

The Dutch who followed the Portuguese in Maritime trade had to face stiff resistance in Malabar. It was this hostility that compelled the Zamorin to revive the Marakkar Tradition in 1667.

The British who occupied Malabar in 1799, cleverly exploited the indigenous expertise. The British Government started a teak plantation at Nilambur, the upper Basin of Chaliyar River in 1845 to make available sufficient quantity of Teak for Railways and for Bombay, Bassin dockyards. A series of MPPF (Malabar Preservation of Private Forest) Acts were promulgated, which imposed restriction on felling certain variety of trees. The British ship-Building in India progressed so well that "It rivalled any in the world". As a result, the British ship-building industry declined at home and the building companies and yard owners got a law enacted that 80 per cent of the commodities imported to Britain should be brought in British bottoms.

This also gave rise to the Teak-Oak controversy in 19th century. If canon fire is hit on Oak built ship, it splinters away while of Teak would cause only hole which can be repaired.

It is believed that in the battle of Trafalgar, Admiral Nelson had teak-built ships of Beypore under his command.

A continuous history of ship-building tradition was the heritage of Malabar, while the rest of the centres witnessed ups and downs of the rise and decline of the trade and political power.

In certain cases, related to shipbuilding, not the direct meaning of the word but local usage was nearer to truth. A scholar from Tamil Nadu presented a paper in a seminar where among the best timber for ship building he included Nutmeg. Anybody who is acquainted with nutmeg tree knows that it is a soft tree, not at all strong. Its branches will break when it is slightly bent, and never grows in girth to be sawed for planks and withers when it is old. The mistake was the result of translating the word 'Jathi'. Jathi is name for nutmeg in Malayalam. It also means kind, type of variety. Jathi in colloquial usage is the name for teak-also meaning best type (Jathi) of Timber. Jathi alone is used to refer to teak. But no dictionary meaning for Jathi is teak.

Place name studies had been very useful for this study. In the documents (Palm Leaf Manuscripts) of Calicut Grandhavari we come across such important evidences of the year 1667, on the ceremony of conferring the title of 'Kt.mjali Marakkar' on one member of the Marakkar family, in an attempt of Zamorin to revive the Marakkar fighters to repulse the Dutch depredations in Calicut. Dr. N.M.

Namboothiri unfortunately translated Qalandar as 'Commander'. He did not have any idea of Qalandari Sufi Order. Here without knowledge of Sufi Orders, the present writer should have adopted the translation. But Qalanders were Sufi Brotherhood of Marakkar pledged to fight unto death.

The presence of Karuvanthimthi (Island of Blacksmiths) in Beypore is a sufficient indication of blacksmith settlement and use of iron in ship-building.

Many discussions with people engaged in timber business, Toni, Therappam and Ship-building yards, with owners Mestris and Odayis had been useful for the study.

The paper reports of Traditional Ships rebuilt has been used.

The Kappappattu (ship song) and a philosophical work was very useful for the study. This work is composed in Jasari languages–a mixture of Arabic, Persian, Tamil, Kannada, and Telugu. Jasari from Jazira (Island) in Arabic.

The wall paintings of mosque at Areacode with minute details of an elegant ship including the steps of ladder from one storey to another, each being given specific use was of unique value for the study.

Works of eminent scholars in the field like K.S. Mathew etc. was helpful for a comparative study.

When the work is completed, a strong conviction remains that more materials and information can still be gathered on the subject.

CHAPTER-1

Ship-building

One hundred and fifty of the hundred and eighty member states of U.N. are coastal and two-third of world's population lives within 100 miles of the coast. This means that a very large proportion of world's economic, industrial, social and political activity is carried out in area on land and sea extending 200 nautical miles.

Malabar, the northern part of Kerala (sometimes the whole of Kerala as Arab geographers called it) is a narrow coastal strip with Arabian sea on the west and western ghats on the east, enjoying heavy monsoon and with 42 big and small rivers. This means that all human activities of the area is connected with the sea and Maritime life. A survey of such maritime traditions of Medieval Malabar is the objective of this study. An indepth study of ship-building tradition in different centres of Malabar is attempted here.[1] The study is mainly based on field-work.

The very name Malabar itself is derived from Maritime contact. Shamshullah Qadiri has established that the word is combination of two words. The Dravidian word 'Mala' (hills) is added with Persian word 'Baar' (land) making 'Malabar', land of hills (hilly land). Thus, the name itself is an evidence for Persian contact from time immemorial. Hwi cao's (Ca. 712 AD) comments on Persians, show that firstly the Persians were by nature bent on commerce. Secondly,

Persians sailed to Cylon in search of precious stones. Thirdly, the purchase of silk piece goods and the like made the Persian sails travel straight to Canton. By AD 727, Persian Navigation was at its height, which seems to have started long before. Persians had taken over Sassanid navigation and initiated Arabs to eastern trade.[2] Romans[3] and later Arabs used the word with minor variations.[4]

Only causal reference to ship-building on Malabar coast was made by travellers, until the arrival of Portuguese, who out of their natural interest, tried to understand the merits and demerits of ships built in Malabar, comparing the material, technology and cost with their own as it had vital significance for trade.

Recently, a team of scholars based in Delhi, took up a project for study of ship-building under NISTADS (Delhi) with which the present writer was also associated as Regional co-ordinator. But the study concentrated in Bombay. Gujarat, Laccadives and Malabar Coast with thousands of years of heritage was not included in the study.

In a discussion of scholars on timber for ship-building, it was sorrowfully revealed that people were ignorant of the size and variety of timber in the rainforests of Malabar and the contention was that large size timber was imported from Africa.[5]

The study is mainly based on field-work in the selected ship-building centres of Malabar Valapattanam, Beypore and Ponnani for various reasons. It is only in "Ponnani where an active maritime community of people, ready recruits for sailing exists. Again it is only in Beypore where large Urus are constructed and the main Khalasi community exists. In Valapattanam alone the big ships called Vanchi or Vallam is constructed. Closer interaction with these groups have revealed hitherto unknown curious, interesting and unrecorded traditions of maritime people.

A scholar recently has recorded from various sources several types of ships built in the south west and south east coasts. Different types of crafts were built from Thiruvananthapuram to Kasargode for different purposes like movement from one region to another, trade and communication, transportation of passengers and cargo, fishing, merry making, racing, naval fight and other purpose.

Different types of ships known on south-west coast were;

1. Toni (both small and big)
2. Pataku/Patav/Kallapadaku
3. Ambi
4. Timil
5. Marakkalam
6. Chonku (The big ship of China)
7. Chambrani (The small ship of China)
8. Pathemari
9. Chonadan (The small pandildmppal)
10. Odivallam ll.Vanchi
12. Vallam
13. Odam
14. Plavam
15. Chamba
16. Paru
17. Pottam
18. Varkas
19. Ottukalam
20. Chiri
21. Patram
22. Tarani
23. Chivata
24. Uru/Uruva
25. Kalivallangal
26. Palliyodam
27. Iruthikuthi Vallam
28. Churulan Vallam
29. Valar
30. Parua
31. Kottam
32. Koapakam
33. Kolam
34. Champakam[6]

Among the above ships, familiar and constructed in Malabar were:

1. Maram[7]
2. Toni
3. Veppu Toni
4. Ottadi Vallam[8]
5. Vanchi/Manchi
6. Vallam
7. Muri Vallam
8. Kettu Vallam
9. Charaldcuvallam[9]
10. Kavuvallam
11. Chundan Vallam[10]
12. Ottakkori Vallam
13. Vishuvala Vallam[11]
14. Machua
15. Uru

List of big ships used for sea transportation

1. Arumas (big ships)
2. Anayodi (big ships) (Ana: Elephant = f or transportation of elephants)
3. Odi
4. Kappal (Crossing the ocean)
5. Kettumaram
6. Kettuvalam (Transporting cargo)
7. Kevukappal (Transporting cargo)
8. Kevu Toni (The passenger vessel)
9. Kodikappal
10. Changadam
11. Padagu
12. Pathel
13. Pathemari
14. Marakkalam[12]
15. Vanchi Valar (The kappal used by people of Valarapattanam)

Ship -building engulfed a whole economic and social system. It required assemblage at one centre, of a variety of raw materials brought from many places. Presupposes an extensive and efficient system of communication, co-operation of large bodies of workers from the tribals who construct roads on steep hills to the Khalasis who launch the ship. Workers, each specialized in distinct crafts, all acting together in accordance with a common plan, under a centralized direction. Ship- building activity involved collective attempt and united efforts of different social classes, some of them as follows:

1. Tribals familiar with interior forests who proposes and work on timber, dragging paths or roads.
2. Wood cutters, who move to the interior forests for months together under one contractor/agent.
3. Makers of iron implements, from axes to rasping saws near forests.
4. The hand sawers of large logs.
5. Suppliers of groceries for the temporary sheds for wood cutters, etc.
6. Buffalo and Bullock carts to carry or drag large logs to Anayelu (Track of elephants) which is used by elephants for many years, a natural selection of animal instinct.
7. Temporary tea shops and hotels near worksites.
8. Therappam/Changadam workers.
9. Tea/cattering centres on river banks for Therappam workers– often small house holds.
10. The timber merchants.
11. Suppliers of special timbers for masts etc.
12. Capital investors.
13. Owners of ship-building guards.
14. Odayis, skilled capenters.
15. Kammalis. Manual labourers/helpers.
16. Raw-nail and Anchor producers.
17. Coir producers for sewn plank boats.
18. Suppliers of sardine oil, cashew oil, punna oil or shark oil.

19. Producers and suppliers of lime.
20. The caulkers.
21. The priests for Pooja and Mullas for prayer.
22. The khalasi community for launching ships.
23. The crew of various order.
24. The owners of crafts.[13]

The components of this ship-building activity worked so well that it won the appreciation of European Travellers. Portuguese Historian Barros noted on sheathing of Junks with Bitumen compound from slaked-lime and fish oil. This was both warm and waterproof. Barros' friend Fernao Peres de Andrade introduced the system to Portugal.[14] The excellence and economic advantage was so tempting that Barbossa noted in all the cities he visited on Malabar and Eastern coast 'Moorish traders who possessed either good number of vessels' or owners of "great ships after the fashion of Meca".[15] He recorded that the traders when they return from red sea, bring other moors who also get ships constructed and settle in Calicut. He got four ships constructed in Calicut (Beypore), two for Chettis of Calicut and two for Muslim merchants of Mecca under his supervision around 1515. The coast of construction in Calicut and Lisbon was 1:2 and the finest timber for ship-building in the world, the Teak of Malabar was Beypore's most favourable factor.

The European observers provide important information on material, types and variety of ships. This tradition of ship-building has influenced even folklore of the region. A Sufi Poem 'Kappappattu', ascribed to a 13th century author, depicts human body as ship, soul as the captain, and god as port of destination with details of life similar to a voyage in the sea.

The political upheavals influenced the rise and fall of many of the trade centres in medieval times. The unalterable factor, namely the availability of timber and workers helped some of the centres to sustain. Beypore near Calicut was the centre which has a continuous tradition of ship-building. This study is concentrating on materials, workers and technology based on the observations of ship-building in Beypore and other ports.[16]

Beypore is on the mouth of River Chaliyar. Nainar identified 'Shaliyat' of Arabs with Beypore. But there were these ancient towns of Chaliyam and Beypore on either side of the confluence. The Romans, Chinese and Arab travellers mention Chaliyam[17] and Abulfida makes an important statement that its inhabitants are Jews.

Finest quality of timber was easily available in Beypore. The rain forests which formed the upper basins of the river enabled an endless supply of timber which helped Beypore to develop as a centre of ship-building.

The requirement of timber for plank built ships was varied and many. The Pandi (Keel) required a strong, hard and heavy timber. The Vari (ribs) frame, on which the strength and durability of the ship depends had to be stronger and if possible should be essentially of teak and mast should be straight, strong but of light weight. Timber with all these qualities arrived inBeypore by Therappam.[18] Therappam was not only the cheapest means of transport, but logs in any size could be carried to the yards which was otherwise impossible.

At the forest felling sites, builders ordered certain timbers in specific size.

Various types of ships were built in Beypore. Some of them were

1. Bomb = Boom
2. Padavu
3. Bireek
4. Kottiya
5. Sambook
6. Bahla
7. Pathemar

Materials required at various stages of construction, and in case of timber, different types of timber with specific qualities were readily conveyed to Beypore.

The Pandi (Keel) of the ships was made of Karimaruthu (Terminalia crenulata). The length of the keel was taken to be the length of the ship[19] and had to be less than 100ft.[20] The Vari (rib), frame as far as possible in natural 'V' shape could be procured in required size from Karimaruthu or Maruthu, especially from Pilavu, Jackfruit tree (***Artocarpus integrifolios***). The natural 'V' shape was stronger than any other joints. Handsawn teak alone was used for planks. It was the teak that gave pre-eminence to Beypore in ship-building.

The quality of teak grown in the upper basins of Chaliyar tempted the British Administration to start the Conolly's teak plantation in 1850.[21] The British administration also promulgated a series of MPPF Acts (Malabar Preservation of Private Forest Acts) for preservation of certain varieties of timber. Teak was also exported as timber to the building centres of West Coast.[22] From the 17-19th century, English ship-building was concentrated in Bombay. The Bombay Dockyard in 1775 rivalled any in Europe. The export of teak has been attested by the Arab geographers. Yaqut and Qazwini mention huge and tall teak tree in Kulam.[23] One British expert James Kyd observed "Malabar teak was certainly the best timber in the world" for ship-building.

According to Digby staple commodities produced in India included teak wood with its superior virtues for ship-building which had been used since Pre-Islamic times for ships plying in the Persian Gulf and the Arabian Sea. With other woods teak was in demand for pillars, beams and roofing in Persian Gulf and South Arabia.[24]

Slender, straight, strong but light, tapering to top, pali was best suitable timber for mast. Pali (***Palaqim Elepticum***) was abundant in Wynad forests, not in Nilambur.

Cordage at various stages was done with Coir. The raw iron nails were locally manufactured. These days, industrial units manufacture nails and also cast anchor. The only material not locally available in Beypore was cotton wicks used in caulking.

The carpenters engaged in ship-building were called Odayis. (Odam = boat, Odayi = boat builder). These traditional builders claim that their ancestors were the people who built Odam for Ceraman Parumal (The King of Kerala who ruled upto 1221 AD) to go to Mecca.[25] Some of them are also temple builders.

According to tradition, the king pleased with the skill in building Odam presented 'Pattum Valayum' (silk and golden bangle) to a carpenter and gave him the honorific title of "Odayi". The elder member (Mestri) of a family employs his sons and grandsons with a group of others in a work. Every important work, including joining planks is done with Mestri's permission. He gives the list of requirements which are readily supplied by builder's agents.

He also fixes the wages for builder's agents. He fixes the wages for which the workers are categorised as 'A', 'B', 'C' in accordance their labour output and skill.

Mestris keep their basic drawings. When the size of the ship is fixed, the measurement of frame is calculated and a platform with joined planks is made at one side of the Chappa (Shed).

The Odayis had to be free from vices, mind and memory should always be clear a maxim which they have respectfully maintained.

They have developed technology with experience of generations, saving much labour and bringing the ship-building to perfection.

For Pandi (Keel) a single piece of Karimaruthu is preferred. Joints in the keel are fastened by pulling 'Pantham' (resin of ***Canarium Sprictum***) and cloth-in the joints to prevent leakage. The first and second planks near the keel 'ottupalaka' (close plank) and 'thathila' (Thazhathe Palaka-bottom plank) were earlier made of Ben teak (***legestremia lanceolata***). Since the timber would swell in water it would make the keel watertight. Timber with natural curve and bends was preferred so that the number of joints could be lessened.

The search for suitable timber saved labour, avoided unnecessary weight[26] and prevented wastage of timber.

Odayis had a technique for bending teak planks with Olive oil. At first Olive oil is applied to teak planks and heated. The plank absorbs the whole oil. The process is repeated and then oil oozes out when it is slightly bent in required angles.

Kalpathu (caulking) is done for making the ship leak proof.[27] Cotton wicks dipped in Punna oil (***Calloplyllum Inophyllum***) was thrust between the planks. These days, groundnut oil and Margosa oil are also used since Punna oil is not available.

When the planks are joined, the cuttings are arranged to touch three varis. The topmost plank (Aruthippalaka, Amthi = last) was joined in tongue and groove method.

The head of iron nails was covered before chopra (embalming) with pantham, oil and lime boiled together.

The last stage is chopra or embalming animal fat boiled with lime coated all over the ship outside. Fish oil is smeared inside. Arabs use fish oil in abundance and hence the Arab owned ships are more durable.

When smaller boats, canoes etc. were made with cheap timber, cashew oil is used for enbalming to protect them from sea worms.

The cost of a ship cannot be calculated since it is kept a secret due to many reasons.

The durability of a ship also could not be assessed since no records were available. The Mestris claim that ships built fifty or sixty years ago are now being brought for repair.

These days, ships are constructed for fitting engines though they too have mast and would depend on favourable wind. The Amaram (rear) is specially designed to adjust the fan of the engine. Engines are fitted abroad, they are towed to Gulf countries.

Beypore has a continuous history of ship-building from ancient times. Some of the ship-building families are moving to Mangalore etc. for various reasons. Cheap Malayesian timber is also another reason.

Ship-building industry in Beypore is the culmination of our history, culture, social organisation and technology and a rich heritage of the land.

A problem widely discussed while talking of ship-building in 16th century elsewhere in India is the Indian response to European Technology. A comparison of technology, superiority inferiority or adoption naturally comes up. It is generally believed, as noted by Marcopolo, that ships constructed on either side of Peninsular India were "Sewen like clothes with twine" and if the twine breaks anywhere there is a breach indeed".[28]

It is argued that it was after European contact that Indians began to use iron nails. We know that Chinese used iron in their ships long before the appearance of the Portuguese in Asian waters. On the 29th regional year of Akbar (1593), Abul Fasal gives details of a ship constructed on the banks of the Ravi on Emperor's order. Incidentally this is the only documentation of this nature for an Indian ship so far available in the entire Persian literature. We are told that 2936 pieces of big planks and 468 maunds (Akbari) and two sers of iron went to it. 240 carpenters and blacksmiths worked on her.[29] In Malabar there was no dearth of iron. Even the Megalithic burials have iron implements. Old settlements had blacksmith tradition, many place names indicate presence of iron or iron ore. In Beypore, the other side of the river is still known as "Karuvanthumthi", Island/settlement of blacksmiths, which shows that from very ancient times there had been large settlements of blacksmiths. Why should there be such a large settlement of blacksmiths in a place where there was no greater demand for agricultural implements? Close at hand to the ship-building centre, these people were obviously preparing iron implements for ships. Crude nails to join the vari (frame) and required types to join the planks were prepared. Anchors must have also been cast.[30]

During the 16th century, the Europeans whom Malabar came into contact were the Portuguese. There was no question of mutual influence since the relation was hostile. Especially in Beypore since the Chaliyam Fort was founded in 1522 till its destruction in 1573 by the Zamorin- Mappila alliance, the relation was not friendly. Beypore also had Marakkar settlements. Yet there is every possibility that ship-building continued. Because in 16th century though the Muslims of Calicut lost monopoly of high sea trade, other parties in Indian Ocean were allowed to carry on trade as the Portuguese depended highly on revenue from trade in markets of their control and even attracted Muslim merchants to Malacca. So the Surat, Cutch and Persian-gulf regions had unhampered trade where the Beypore ships were in demand. Until Surat under the Mughals with European assistance developed a ship- building centre, and later the establishment of British ship-construction in Bombay, Beypore maintained this envious position. With the establishment of Bombay Company, sawn timber and logs began to be exported from Beypore. Teak was so much in demand that it was to meet the demand of Bombay ship-building yard and for Railways that the British Government started a teak plantation in Nilambur under the supervision of Collector H.V Conolly [31] in 1850. As early as 1775 it has been noted that Bombay dockyard "Rivalled any in Europe".

The construction cost per ton of European ships in 17th century was calculated at Rs.54, while for Indian ships construction cost was between Rs.30-40 per ton.[32]

The Calicut ship-builders had no chance of interaction with Portuguese, though the captives might have been in service on board. It has been noted that, often in the Portuguese vessels there had been very few white men. No evidence of cannon mounted ships is available. It was not possible in Beypore because of the Portuguese Fort of Chaliyam in 16th century. More over the Calicut Navy under Kunhali Marakkars were not resorting to straight canon fire. But were using small war parrows in hideouts to ambush and dash like blood hounds, cause maximum damage and retreat to shallow waters and rivulets where Portuguese were not able to chase them. This does not mean that Calicut, Navy was consisted of war parrows only. We find Zamorins, Navy fighting Portuguese off Gujarat with the Navy of Pasha of Egypt under Mir. Hussain and Sulthan of Turkey under Sidi Ali Reis. We also note Marakkars fighting in Ceylon and on eastern coast often upto Orissa, and protecting Hajj pilgrims or escorting Mercantile flotilla. These operations on high seas would not have been possible without canon mounted ships.

The Carpenters, Varthema observed, "Join the planks so well that they Keep trout water most excellently".[33] The indigenous method of rabetting was so perfect that it needed no caulking. Yet caulking (Kalpathu) was done. Cotton wicks dipped in Punna oil (***Callophyllum Inophyllum***) was thrust between the planks. Chopra (embalming) was the last stage of construction. Animal fat[34] boiled with lime was coated all over the ship outside. Fish oil was smeared inside. Arabs used fish oil in abundance and Arab owned ships were more durable.

Smaller boats with cheaper timber were embalmed with cashew oil, perhaps the only European influence in ship-building in Beypore.

The durability of a ship could not be assessed. The Mestris

(Traditional overseers of ship construction) claim that ships built fifty or sixty years before were being brought for repair. Now the repair is being done in centres in the gulf under migrant Odayis and imported teak.

The Odayis whose ancestors, it is claimed, constructed ships for the Ceraman Perumal to go to Mecca (ca 1220?) are the traditional builders. Since the entire families takes to the job, wages are fixed according to labour output. They keep a drawing on joined planks in one side of the chappa (shed). Odayi tradition required to be free from vices, so that mind and memory should always be clear.

Any study of ship-building will be incomplete without reference to Khalasis. The origin and meaning of the name is not theme of discussion. Khalasis were the people who launched the ship. Foreign accounts have description of the use of elephants for launching.[35] It was a festive occasion for the natives. All the assembled gave a helping hand. The use of ropes and pulley continued. Khalasis were a category of skilled labourers. Their chief was called Gumti and their duty was to bail out water collected in the ship during a storm.[36]

They did all types of manual labour on the ship. They had mastered the use of capstan, pulleys and cables and could be used forlaunching.[37] We do not know when actually capstan came in to use in Malabar. Khalasis put huge loges of Mango tree on either side and cause the ship to slid on that. It goes to the credit of these people that it were they who lifted the train from water with their capstan and pulleys when all the modern machineries failed. Khasi is another word of Maritime origin that formed into a functional society later.

Reference

1. No serious work on ship-building on the Malabar coast is made except a few survey papers.
2. Hadi Hassan, ***History of Persia Navigation***, p. 103-4.
3. Manibar.
4. Malaibar, Malibar, Malabar often error of transcription. Six writers Sulaiman, Yaqut, Dimashqi, Abu. Fida, Idrisi and Qazwini mention Malabar S.M.H Nainar ***Arab Geographers knowledge of South India***, Madras (1942), p. 56.
5. The discussion took place in a. seminar organized by the Institute of

Oceanography, Goa.

6. Different styles and designs of Kerala vessels. Greeshmalatha A.P. in K.N. Ganesh (ed.) ***Exercises in Modern Kerala History,*** Sahithya Pravarthaka Co-operative Society, Kottayam (2012), pp. 43-47.
7. Earliest form of boat where light woods of a special shape tied together, used for fishing in raging seas.
8. Dug out of single piece of timber, small.
9. For cargos (Charakku)
10. For racing and for fast conveyance in emergency like war.
11. Canoes from which a fisherman cast fishing nets.
12. A.P. Greeshmalatha, ***op. cit.,***
13. Information from interaction with various groups in the profession.
14. C.R. Boxer, ***Jo.aode Barros N.D.*** (1980), p. 108.
15. The Book of Duarte Barbosa, Vol. 2, Haldyut Society Second Series (1921), p. 142.
16. The field study was first undertaken for a research paper ***History of Traditional Navigation,*** Tamil University of Tanjarur (1988) pp. 157-64)
17. lbn-Battuta mentions Chaliyam as "a most beautiful town", H. A. R Gibb, ***Travels in Asia and Africa,*** p. 240.
18. Hundreds of logs tied together made floating and carried down stream.
19. The actual length of the ship will be 7-15 ft. in the Aniyam (front) and 10-25 ft. in the Amaram (rear).
20. When length of the Pandi exceeds 100 ft. many rules become applicable which the builders wanted to avoid. If the ship was to operate in India only there was no such restrictions. But most of the bigger ships built in Beypore were on orders from abroad.
21. This plantation is still continued by the Govt. of India. A few trees planted in the beginning are preserved. In this group is the Biggest planted teak sighted in the world, on the opposite side of Forest Timber Depot of Nilambur.
22. After the loss of American Colonies there was a dirth of ship-building timber. In 19th century when English ship-building in India had concentrated in Bombay the comparative price of teak in India and Oak in England was 1:2.
23. S. M. H Nainar, ***op.cit.,*** p. 206.
24. Tapan Ray Chaudhari and Irfan Habib (Ed.). ***The Cambridge Economic History of India*** (1982, p. 14)
25. The tradition is that the last ruler of Cera dynasty Converted to Islam, "secretly ordered to build a ship", and then left to Mecca. Kerallolpathi, Kerala Pazhama etc. for the tradition in detail. Recent studies have established that the last ruler of second Cera Dynasty ruled up to 1121 and with him the empire fragmented. The traditional works characterize them as 'partitioned' by the last ruler.
26. From 1982-91 there was a strike which with the Iran-Iraqi war, paralysed Beypore.

When· Mestris refused to accept the terms of yard owners they took service of well experienced workers to execute the work. Only one ship was thus built which had to be later rebuilt by Mestris.

27. In Kalpathu a slight European influence is seen. Earlier Varthema observed that the builders "join the planks so perfectly that they do not need caulking", though not fully correct.
28. Yule, ***Cathay and the way tither*** 11, p.66.
29. Abdul Fazal, ***Akbarnama*** iii. pp. 651-52
30. Varthema (1503) who made close observation of ship-building in Calicut recorded, "They use an immense quantity of iron nails in Indian ships". Varthema p. 152.

    Even earlier (1501) Cabral was given the information that ships of south-west were made with iron nails. W.B. Greenly. ***The Voyages of Pedro Alvares Cabral to Braziland India***, p. 105.
31. Conolly was later killed by the Mappilas in his Bunglow in Calicut in retaliation for the banishment of Mamburam Sayyed Alavi Thangal.
32. The value of the ship was calculated on the sale price when the ship was rejected for reasons, inexplainable under compulsion. So actual cost must be higher.
33. Varthema, p. 152.
34. Probably there was no dearth of animal fat because Malabar had large population consuming meat.
35. W.B. Greenly, ***op.cit.***, p. 105.

    Varthema in 1503 and Pyrard in 1610 had seen elephants launching and pulling ships.
36. AJ Qaisar, ***Indian Response to European Technology and Culture***, Delhi (1982), p. 32.
37. Abdul Fazal has noted "It took ten days for 1000 person to launch her in the river" ***Akbarnama*** iii, p. 652.

CHAPTER-II

Rebirth of Medieval Traditions in Ship-building

Beypore was famous as a ship-building centre some three thousand years ago. Three adjacent ports in Malabar, Kadalundi (Tynidis of Romans) and Beypore (Phohar as Romans knew it) within a radius of 10 kms were important trading centres. Kadalundi today is only a fishing village while Beypore and Chaliyam still possess remnants of the glorious past.

Chaliyam was famous for its particular cloth of loose texture. The cloth is known as Chaliyam Mundu (Chaliyam cloth). Chaliyan (Shaliya) is the community of weavers too. The joint authors of Arabi-Malayala Sahithyam are of opinion that the cloth which covered the Mummys of Pharohas was from Chaliyam. We know that the spice and incenses used for prayers in Egypt were probably brought from Malabar. Spice oils were used for Mummifying the dead. The texture of Mummys and the Chaliyam cloth is similar as I have personally verified. This is not an attempt to establish any tall claim. But the loose texture of the Chaliyam cloth will allow trickling oil inside any number of folds of the cloth. It is said Chaliyam was also one of the centre where Jews migrated on the invasion of Nabuchad Nasa.[1]

There is also a tradition that once a sun temple existed in Chaliyam. Beypore is on the right bank (and Chaliyam on the left bank of the river mouth where Chaliyar (River of Chaliyam) flows to the sea.

The strategic importance of Chaliyam can be understood that in 1542 the Portuguese with pressure on the Zamorin erected a Fort in Chaliyam which was captured and demolished by the joint forces of Zamorin and Mappilas in 1573, marked the beginning of the end of Portuguese attempt to colonize India and monopolizing spice trade.

It has been proved that in the remains of Ur and in the Palace of Barsarim Rud of Emperor Nebuchad Nasar (BC 604-562), teak has been found. The best teak was available only in Nilambur and Wynad which could be exported only from Beypore.

As of today timber for ship building was exported from Beypore. Arab geographers have noted that ships were built in Malabar and sold in gulf countries.

In the battle of Trafalgar of 1806, British Navy had ships of teak constructed in Beypore. It was the superior qualities of teak that tempted Britishers to start teak plantation of Nilambur in 1845, for the purpose of shipyards of Surat and Bassein and for railways.

Beypore became famous all over the world and people from various countries came to Beypore to get ancient and medieval ships of their imagination constructed. Though in quantum these new works were smaller, they once again made the skill of Beypore builders famous all over the world.

The Dhows of Beypore was renowned. Two youths from Germany decided to conduct a voyage along the route of Vasco Da Gama in a ship built on the model of Vasco Da Gama's Ship, sailing with wind. They came to know of this centre of Dhow construction, from a book, where they felt a ship of their imagination can be built.

During August 1979 they landed in Calicut and contacted Baramis an important ship-building 'company with their model and requirement.

Within some months, got constructed the ship of their dream. This strong ship of Sambook type, left Beypore on world tour on the routes of Vasco Da Gama of 1498. They traversed the route of return of Gama and named their ships after him. The ship was launched on 16 March 1980 and left Kappad to Lisbon on the same route.

It was a great event and P.M. Aboobacker, the Minister for Public Works and Shanmukam, the Minister for Ports attended the launching ceremony. The 1200 year old history was being reenacted. The ancient trade route of Persian gulf-Hongkong-China was traversed by these adventures.

The launching of Al–Qaseer in 1983 was another important landmark in the history of ship-building. It was a pleasure boat constructed for Hussain Marafi, a millionaire of Kuwait, by the Baramis. In 1915 another ship of the same type was built in Beypore which was named 'Mohammedi First'. The ship Al-Qaseer was therefore called by the name Muhammedi Second' too. The ship Al-Qasar had a Restaurant where 58 people could dine at a time. It had also a coffee saloon for 20 people and dock for Sunbath. The ship was handed over to Hussain Marfi by Minister Vayalar Ravi on 5th April 1983 in Beypore.

Many people other than Arabs, from various countries had come to Beypore for constructing ships. Captain Tim Severin, head of Ocean studies from Oman in April 1983 and Major Edward Christopher from Switzerland in 1985 were some of them.

In 1980s Beypore had earned world wide reputation when a strike broke out as a bolt from the blue in 1983, which lasted for eight years. Arab investors lost their money. The construction companies could not deliver and were at loss. Thousands of labourers lost their works. By the time the strike ended the construction of Urus had been shifted elsewhere. Baramis had been in the field for 200 years. P.I. Ahammed Koya and sons are newcomers with a history of 70 years, who also construct ships of traditional types of Beypore.

During June 1977 the AI Basheer Co. constructed a pleasure boat for Shaikh Saqar bin al-Qasim, the ruler of U.A.E. This was a present to the king by his close friend, Ibrahim Salima, who was an industrialist of UAE. The ship was given the name of the king itself. This was a floating palace with A/c, rooms platform for casting lines and luxurious dining hall.

The construction of 'Sur' was another important event of Beypore. Sur was constructed for the German Citizen Lamley by Al-Basheer and Co. Sur is a small port of Muscat, and Lamley happened to see the small beautiful crafts in the port. He learnt that these ships were mostly built in Beypore. Lamley reached Calicut in September 1991. He was a lover of sea and voyage, who wanted a small ship with all convenience for his world tours, to be anchored in any small port. Being convinced that Beypore is the only place to convert his dream into reality, he approached Al-Basheer Co. who constructed the ship in two months at a cost of rupees 9 lacks. Though it was fitted with engine it could also travel with sail spread. In November 99, Lamley set sail on his world tour from Beypore.

The building of 'Kiyenki', a ship built perfectly on 3000 years old ancient Sumerian model, was another important event in the history of ship-building. The ship was constructed to retrace the ancient silk route from China to Mesopotamia. It was constructed without using machine and iron. This was a sewn plank built ship on the ancient Sumerian model for Akira Iwatha, a Navigator of Michayiline Shipping Company of Japan. He got information on Beypore ships from Sumerian tables, which he came across in Lube Museum of Pairs. His intention was to traverse the ancient silk route in the Sumerian ship,[2] passing through Karachi, Oman, Bahrain and Basra to reach Mesopotamia, to come back along the same route and preserve the ship in Calicut. A society for preservation of Sumerian ships was formed in Calicut under the chairmanship of the then Vice-Chancellor Dr. Iqbal Hasnain.[3] The ship was sewn with fine coconut fibres, using only manpower and carpenters tools in the famous Al-Basheer company.

The dreams of explorer Akira Iwatha could not be realized as his ship sank in China 100 kms off the Japanese coast and the whole crew was rescued by Japanese Helicopters. By the time Akira Iwatha had travelled 6700 Nautical miles in 117 days.

Tim Severin of Ireland, an adventurous sailor has paid glowing tribute to Beypore-Calicut ship-builders in his book, The ***Sindbad Voyage.*** He writes, Today the trade with Arabs in Calicut has shrunk to two houses, the Barami's and Koyas (P.I. Ahammed Koya and Sons). These are two houses facing the sea, with a yard and many sheds behind.

In these sheds are stocked the Aalath (ropes). The nails for Urus, the oil Cheruvi (for embalming) and handmade anchors. The long sitouts are the life of these companies. The Arabs spend days and enjoy evenings on these sitouts, sipping tea or 'Qahwa'. Many beggars for alms also gather outside. These two trade links with Arabs are influential among Muslims. The heads of these houses contact trade and transactions. Timber and spices, forest products and coir etc. are exported. Abdul Qadir Baramis, the head of Baramli's is an experienced and efficient business man. By god's grace he has seven brothers. But nothing goes without his consent, and that is the tradition. As of old, he knows all about the traders, timber and Uru constructors of Malabar, much than anyone else. I asked him whether a ship on the ancient model can be constructed with Timber and rope (sewn). He said it is not possible to construct on ancient model but in Beypore we can build ships with mast from best teak.[4]

The Yusuf Sagar Co. and Jifri and Karim Company are also ship-builders and traders centred in Beypore.

The construction of the ships on the ancient and Medieval model especially the sewn plank boats points to the ancient tradition of Beypore. Akira Iwatha of Japan who captained the 'Sumerian ship', a sewn plank built ship, said in a conference in Calicut that his information of Beypore was gained from the Museum of Pairs, derived from Sumerian tables. Another important evidence of Sumerian contact was the word 'Karimkallu' for granite in Sumerian language, which is the same in Malayalam even today.

This is another glowing example of the excellence of "Malabar teak", used and exported from Beypore, brought down from the upper basins of Chaliyar especially Nilambur and also of the Odayis of Beypore.

Fortunately I had occasions to interact with people involved in the long process of felling trees, rowing Therappam, Sawers, Odayis (Carpenters of ship) Khalasis and the above mentioned shipyard owners. One of my relatives was the biggest supplier of timber to Calicut and Beypore, who introduced me to all these people and enabled long and free interaction and survey.

Reference

1. At least one Arab geographer Abulfida while describing the city of Chaliyam noted 'The inhabitants are mostly jews'.
2. I had occasion to interact with Capt. Akira Iwatha in Beypore as I had decided to concentrate in Beypore ship-building.
3. As the head of the Department of History and a member of Calicut heritage initiative. I was associated with the construction and launching of the ship at every stage.
4. Tim Severin: ***The Sindbad Voyage***, pp. 33.34

CHAPTER-III

Economy–Market Oriented

A flourishing and healthy system of exchange existed in Medieval Malabar. It was a semi-barter system. Men of various profession practiced their vocation producing their utensils for the society which they exchanged for other products, mostly paddy. Every village produced paddy either once, twice or thrice in the wetlands according to the availability of rain, type of soil and variety of seed. Even dry land in rainy season produced best regional variants of paddy. In fact paddy used to be the medium of exchange. Peasant labourers were paid a certain measure of paddy as wages. A carpenter may exchange his products with a black smith and a washerman, will exchange any of them for paddy. Grocers' shops received paddy of the measure calculated to its value in cash. Service personnels like priests and Mullas received their salary as paddy from any household, which a man going round with a gunny bag will collect from each house, twice a year after the two main harvests. Even those who may not have students studying in the local Madrasas would give a measure of paddy when the agent passes by.

There were cash crops which were not generally sold against paddy but against cash or gold. All the foreigners who visited Malabar have noted the special products not procurable elsewhere. The Arab geographers right from Sulaiman to Ibn Battuta have described the markets and merchandise. But they tend to notice only items like pepper spices, timber, Ivory, herbs, pearls, cocoanut, fibre, and dryfish, etc.

The intake was also on the same model. In villages, barter system existed. But pepper, etc. were not exchanged in barter. Peddlers would go round with a gunny bag and his rude balance for weighing or his weighing rod (silver rod) as it was called.

A strange custom is still observed in Malabar. After thrashing the pepper and collecting all the pepper grains, the waste bunches are strewn in the footpath till the main path. The people used to say that it is for the comfort of the travellers so that they will prey for better crops for the farmer. But the practice was originally meant to give information for the peddler passing by that in this house there is pepper, ready to sell, so that he may go in to the house and collect pepper. Another peddler would collect cashew or Arecanut in the same manner.

The weekly markets which were the integral part of rural life also functioned as an avenue of exchange. The shopkeepers of weekly markets carried them by river to the harbour markets.

There were no good roads in Malabar until the Mysorean rulers constructed roads for the movement of the Army especially of cavalry and canons. Even after the Mysorean rule, the pathetic condition of roads was noted by a British woman who toured Malabar in 1808 and noted "The pitiable condition of roads in Malabar, which was also noted by Buchanan earlier.[1] All the main pathways led to ferries. Bullock cart could alone use the roads, that too ending in ferries or to the Big Bazar of Calicut or nearby towns. In Medieval settlements of Malabar, all the roads led to ferry. One important feature was that all the mosques were constructed for the use of river passengers and village people. The main entrance was always on the road to the ferry. In some of the mosques people could perform ablution (ritual cleaning) in the river and attend prayer. The mosque in Areacode referred elsewhere in the chapter on Maritime influence in art, literature and Sufism is one such mosque, where the main entrance is from the ferry and another from the residential area. This is an eighteenth century mosque constructed in traditional architecture with massive wooden pillars and beams and fine carvings.

All the cargo to the ports naturally flowed through rivers and the merchandise back to the villages and small towns of the upper reaches of the rivers.

Bullock carts were advanced method of transport, and the bullock cart owners were rich people of the day, as a Lorry owner or fleet owner in modern times. Bullock carts also served the purpose of a car. Rich people used specially made decorated carriages with shining brass parts and bullocks garlanded with bells and horns mounted with bronze covers. Fine silk clothes were also spread on them. The bullock carts in Medieval times served all the purposes of carriage.

For heavier loads Buffalo carts, which had wheels with larger diameter, bigger in size and loading space were used. These generally were used for transport of timber especially as large logs to the ferries which used to be conveyed in the required original size to the market by 'Therappam' in rainy seasons.[2]

The whole summer these timber logs used to be collected from country side to be floated down on Therappam during rainy season. Buffalo carts were always used in felling areas of auctioned forests. Where Buffalo carts could not operate, Buffalos alone were used to drag large logs with a large number of helpers in uneven lands which gradually developed into tracks, later to be used by bullock carts, gradually to be developed into roads.[3]

Acres of land on river banks sloping to the river were stacked with timber the whole of summer. Some times a single family or more persons owned such temporary timber yards. The owners of such yards (perta)[4] levied rent for keeping timber in their lands.

These logs were being carried to timber yards to be hand sowed for ship-building or to be sawn in size to be exported to building yards of Surat, Bombay or Persian gulf regions.

Larger quantity of commodities were not being carried on the back of animals as in other parts of the country, instead they were carried as head loads. This was specially noted by Ibn-Batuta on his visit to Malabar, which he was destined to traverse from Kollam

(Quilandy) of north to Southern Quilon.[5] On the main routes, hundreds of people moved with head loads. Athanis,[6] wooden, laterite, or granite structures of a man's height were constructed as an offering by locals or a group, or a single individual or family. Large number of such Athanis were seen till modern times on way sides. Most of them, now either demolished by public works department or people. But the place name still remains as Marathani(wooden) Kallathani (of laterite) and Karimkallathani (of granite). Drinking water for animals[7] sambharam (buttermilk) and salted Amla for passengers were freely provided on the way side. A man carrying a gunny bag load also used to carry a bamboo stick of his length. The bamboo stick used to be carried on shoulder and with one end support the weight slightly so that he can do a brisk walk. When the load is put on the Athani he will support the weight on the bamboo stick and take rest. After some time by slightly removing the bamboo stick the load rests perfectly on his head.

Two men used to carry heavier load on ropes hung from a bamboo stick. The bamboo is carried on shoulders. They change shoulders and walk in a half running style since the whole body is free. Though this practice is not common, it is still in practice in the interiors. The author of 'Amini Islands'[8] has given a very good picture of this practice in Amini Islands of Laccadives in his work.

Therappam, as noted elsewhere in this chapter, was the cheapest means of transport of timber. It was not possible to carry timber by road in the size required in ship-building yards. They were brought to the river bank collection centres by timber merchants, which were then sold to wealthy merchants, or owners of petta. The brokers for ship- builders occasionally used to visit such centres where they would purchase the timber and fix their identification marks with a strong iron seal. The Therappam workers used to enter in contract to take them to timber yards. They may start from an upper region and as it floats down, many more timber purchased either by one broker or more used to be added with it. They were identified by the seal. The workers kept ready the logs to be carried in one therappam for specific buyers. There were often one or more Thonis with a therappam or changadam. Therappams moved only during rainy season or just after rain when the river flow was full. This was possible because there were no Dams or barrages barring water transport free movement.

These therappam used to reach the timber yards from tree felling sites in two or three days. The workers would take rest in turn or cook their meals in the Thonis attached in the therappam. Small catering centres were seen on the river banks or near ferries where these workers took their meals. On the rivers in the cold night, these therappam moved with their old 'Fanus'[9] lighted and hung a little high, singing their favourite songs. On return with the Thoni's, they used to carry goods purchased by local grocers or to market places. There were Thoni's which regularly conducted trips in a day or two to bring supplies to the markets and grocers.

A peculiar custom of fixing the price in markets is noted by Varthema, as was practiced till recently in the country sides as I have witnessed. Varthema, the Italian traveller, who made detailed description of the city, market, king, nobles, houses and various castes noted this peculiar custom:

> And when the purchaser and seller wish to make an agreement, they all stand in a circle and the 'Corator' (Broker) takes a cloth and holds it there openly with one hand and with the other hand he takes the right hand of the seller, that is the two fingers next to the thumb, and then he covers with the said cloth his hand and that of the seller, and touching each other with those two fingers, they count from one up to one hundred thousand secretly, without saying 'I will have so much' or 'so much". But in merely touching the joints of the fingers they understand the price and say 'yes' or 'no'. And the broker answers 'no' or 'yes'. And when the broker has understood the will of the seller, he goes to the buyer with the said cloth, and takes his hand in the manner above mentioned, and by the said touching he tells him he wants so much. The buyer takes the finger of the broker and by the said touches says to him "I will give him so much". And in this manner they fix the price".[10]

This practice is still followed in cattle market where the price ranges from hundred to few thousands. They hold the joints in middle, half and full or quarter of the 100 or 1000 in order. Clever and vocal brokers make good amount in market places who comes to the market simply with a Mundu (cloth) on their shoulder or just takes his turban. People stand face to face, not essentially in circles as Vmiham noticed.

In some places they have got code language which the traders and buyers alone understand.

For weighing the articles the local weights and measures were used, as follows.

Kazhanju =
Phalam =
Tulam =
Kandi =
Param or
Bharam

Weights varried from place to place on Malabar coast.[11] The measurement of grains, etc. Nali, Idangazhi and Para were used.

4 or 5 Nali 1 Idangazhi
10 Idangazhi 1 para
7 para 1 Sack/ Gum1y bag
One idangazhi is a little more than one litre.

For measuring oil etc. the lowest unit is kuzhiyal, an iron cup with a long handle, the total is then converted to Nazhi/Nali.

For weighing, things to be used in lesser quality like herbs etc. Kazhanju 12 was the lowest unit. And only for very little quantity or fraction, Kuzhiyal was used.

For weighing, gold simpler balances so small that a gold smith could carry it in his pocket, or folding of his clothes' in waist was used. There Panam and rupee weight was calculated which was counted as 1, ½ or ¼ etc.

The horrible flood of 1948 is still remembered by some. There used to be continuous rain and flood. There was no work. Even goods in stock were finished. The whole area was flooded. People starved, entire people eagerly waited for arrival of provision. The river was in full furry and rage. At last one bold young man said I shall take thoni to Calicut. Is there any body to came with me? Two others joined him. While the whole people prayed with raised hands in tears they waded their ores with Thawakkal 13. They returned the third day, braving the raging river. Such hair-raising traditions point to the importance of river and mariners in the life of the people.

The system of collection of merchandize for ships, their security and operation of medieval high sea trade, which were generally called Arab trade, deserves special attention.

Maritime studies of Medieval times tends to concentrate on Technology of ship-building, trading commodities and communities, trade guilds, merchandise, weights and measures.

How did the system operate? How often did the ships come and go? Who were the traders or people on board are questions not often answered.

Ships plying in Medieval times were under different types of ownership.

(a) Owned and Captained by the Nakhuda[14]
(b) Nakhuda leasing the ship from the owner[15]
(c) Shipowner operating trade, while Nakhuda works as an employee under him
(d) Ships leased and fitted for a specific purpose[16]
(e) Ships bought and fitted for a specific purpose[17]

For the study of organisation and working of trade in Medieval time, we have to depend upon Arab chronicles. Especially of Yemen and South Arabian Coast due to various reasons. Since South Arabian ports were terminal of spice trade, it is quite natural the same system was in operation in Malabar too.

1. Yemen trade emporia had a continuous history of flourishing trade from ancient days till the European period.
2. The trade records are continuous and unbroken till modern times.

3. The Arabs were very keen in preserving papers.[18]
4. It was the confluence of eastern trade. Thus from Mocha on the mouth of red sea to Al-Mirbat in the East it had 33 sea port and 11 riverine ports along River Masilah and a number of ports, though not coastal, but located very near to the sea.

Apart from contact with agents, the news of the departure of a ship was proclaimed in the ports by a public crier as may be seen in Al-Khazraji's history. For example, in 626 AH (1228-29) when on the point of sailing for Egypt, AI Malik al-Masud of the Yemen caused proclamation to be made inviting private merchants to join his convoy to Egypt. Drums were always used in southen Arabia for proclamation. In al-Mukalla, the crier or herald was known as 'almutarrib' and the proclamation 'tatrubah'. The crier used to commence with the stock opening phrase to his proclamation ***awwalan sallu alaihi, wal thaniyan Sallu alaihi wal thalithan sallu alaihi*** (first bless him, second bless him, third bless him) ***yakun Maluma lijaminnas*** (Let it be known to all people) etc[19].

There upon passengers arrived with their merchandise. Ibn Haji reports a most revealing case on shipping between Suez (Bandar al-Suwais) and Jeddah, where hiring of space is discussed, in order to convey a number of people and their baggage, each one having a stipulated quantity of effects specified in an appropriate document.[20] That was how merchandise for a ship was collected, if the owner Nakhuda of the ship was not able to carry his own merchandise a ship full load. We get a similar insight in the 19th century novel of Charles Dickens, where the hero of the novel Dick Whittington worked as a servant boy in the house of a shipowner. One day he was informed of the departure of the ship by the daughter of his master and asked him to send whatever merchandise he owned. He offers his only possession, a cat. During the course of the journey they embark on an Island where they are well received and offered grand banquet by the king. But when food was served hundreds of rats came in and spoiled the food. The captain asked why don't you keep a cat? A cat? They didn't know. The captain said "I have one and presented Dick Whittington's cat. There was no sign of a single rat. The king was astounded and pleased and offered many bags full of gold for the cat. The Novel ends with the usual drama, the boy becomes a millionaire, marries the daughter of his master and later becomes the Lord Mayor of London.

Our interest here is, so many people put on board their wares and entrusted it with the captain or to some others. These people could not only sell the wares but purchase from the market other items which may bring better profit to the owner. A question put to an Alim on the status of law and ***shariah*** is interesting in this regard.

One such question is for a ***fatwa*** (legal opinion) on the lawfulness of using European papers water marked with the picture of animals.

Another ***fatwa*** is indicative of the situation created by the Portugese, but for our purpose, it leads to further findings. The question is about a man "who deposited goods in the hands of another, to sell them in the country to which he was proceeding and for the price to take in return, something where he perceives profit, as is the custom among travellers by the sea. This he did, the goods remaining in his hands for a period of two years or more, for an adequate reason obliging him, to not again meet the owner of the goods to deliver them over to him. There is no dispute that when he returns from his voyage he should deposit it (the goods) with a trustworthy person in a certain port. Then the enemy of the Faith the Frank (Portuguese) seized possession of the vessel laden with the said goods at sea, burning it along with all the said goods it contained. Yet no shortcoming nor any action contrary had proceeded from the person with whom the goods were deposited. Must the said person with whom the goods were deposited be responsible, such being the case; Is his holding of the said goods a safe deposit (***amanah***) or not?[21]

The answer is; If no short coming has proceeded from the said person, he is not liable for the safety of the article deposited.

The relevance of the Fatwa is not the theological status. It points to the fact that there was the custom of entrusting (depositing) merchandise with others, who were also authorized to purchase merchandise with the proceeds from other ports. There was also the custom of entrusting the unclaimed property with certain persons/

agency/officers probably in every port.[22]

There were also agents or brockers[23] for business houses or for a port as such and often specialized goods as in the case of Hindu ***Baniyas***, dealers in textiles in Hadrami markets. The ***Baniyas*** also acted as exchangers of bills and advanced money as loan or on mortgage.

Traders or business groups sent money or bills by Merchant guilds like Karimi (***Kariyam***) or Hanjaman (***Anjuvannam***) as revealed in the study of Geniza records by S. D Goitein[24].

There used to be a fixed time for the arrival and departure of ships. The Almanacs current in the port of Aden showed the exact dates according to solar year for the arrival of each shipping fleet, be it from Africa, India Red sea or Persian gulf at Bandar Aden.

In medieval times, the passengers in a ship in Indian ocean littoral were mainly Muslims though we do very well knew that there had been men of various ethnic, linguistic and nationality and of regional origin. On an Arab ship or in any case a ship plying between Gujarat and Mocha people were mainly Muslims, who were more inclined to a pious and spiritual life on board. Some of the traders themselves were great scholars. There was busy movement of Hajj Pilgrims from Surat to Mocha. Surat was known in Mughul Empire as Bandar-I - Mubaraq (The blessed port) as it was the embarkment port for Hajj. There had been state sponsored and subsidized ships for Hajj. Sometimes even nobles sponsored Hajj ships.[25]

There was the custom among scholars all over the Muslim world to travel to Mecca and Medina to study under the tutelage of great scholars of these countries. We have the example of pious Sufis like Bahauddin Zakariya, the founder of 'Suhrawardi ***SilSilah***' in India performing Hajj and studying in Mecca and Medina. It is quite probable that the disciples or followers of Malik Dinar who was the head of the Madrasa of Hasan-al- Basri, after his death constructed 11 great mosques in important Muslims centers of Malabar around 200 A. H. There had also been adventurers like Ibn Batuta who had been initiated to many Sufi orders and had received Khirka from all of them. The Kazeruni Khanqahs in all trade centers flourished. Mariners had such faith in Kazeruni Sufi order that whenever there was some calamity on the sea the captain of the ship would vow a certiain amount to the Kazerini Sufi Khanqah at his destination?[26] The authorities of the Khanqah were sure of making many such vows and whenever a ship anchored in the port, they used to send their people to receive the amount. This system was so well established that Sprencer Trimmingham calls it a 'a powerful insurance system'.[27]

In the Trade Centres after their days business, it were to these Khanqahs (Sufi hospices) they retired. They were members of such large Sufi brotherhood by virtue of being initiated to the order in some far off lands. In these Khanqahs they spent time in special prayers and Dhikr.[28]

That is why Sprencer Trimmingham calls them 'pious night clubs'. In Malabar A few of them contracted Mutta[29] marriages and generated the nucleus Muslim community of 'Muwalladun', [30] all over the world of which the Mappila Muslims of Malabar are one among them. To give them counsels and spiritual training and consolation from the soul harrowing calamities over the sea the captain of the ship employed pious teachers. Thus developed the community of 'Musliyars'. Musliyars are now a group of religious scholars and Madrasa teachers in Malabar, probably another instance of a maritime functionary turned religious functionary.[31] As a relic of custom even today on auspicious days or for a good catch the fisher folk of Ponnani (all Muslims) take a Musliyar, Mulla or Sayyid in their boat out to the sea for a good catch.[32]

Thus trade in medieval times had a complex system of operation. It was a matter of honesty and trust. Often the owner did not even see the merchandise. He had the role of a capital investor. Muslim communities in port cities, developed many of the social organization, and acted as a powerful medium for formation of cosmopolitan culture. In such cosmopolitan cities trade continued unhampered though the masters changed and that was why while the whole Muslims of interior Malabar rose against Britishers in rebellion in 19th century, Muslims of port cities like Calicut and Tallichery were never effected, an example of cosmopolitan nature and economic significance of trade centers. Many maritime functionaries in the port cities and interior became later titles for community functionaries.

Reference

1. "In Malabar even cattle are little used for the transportation of goods which are generally carried by porters" because of lack of good roads and transport system. F. Buchanan, ***Journey through Mysore Canara and Madras***, p. 741.
2. Interview with old Therappam workers.
3. Facts revealed in long interaction with Bullock Cart and Buffalo Cart owners and helpers who had worked in interior forests.
4. Petta also means a market place, where weekly markets were held, a word of probably telugu origin, commonly used in Tamil and Kannada.
5. In Malabar even cattle are not used for the transportation of goods, which are generally carried by porters" F. Buchannan, ***op.cit.***
6. Athanis were structures raised on way side, where the traveler could set aside his head load al and after some time carry it further, so that he need not wait of a helping hand.
7. Often temples, trusts or individuals kept dug out granite tasks which were safely erected near wells as a deed of charity. A passengers would draw water, quench his thirst and pour the rest of water in to the tank so that the animals may benefit.
8. Itaman, Amini Islands
9. A Muarrab (Arabeised) word for light/lamp that could be carried in Mappila colloquial language. In the painting of the ship referred elsewhere in this work the name for light/lamp is also Fanus. In Malayalam Panees.
10. Varthama, Travels.
11. K.S. Mathew, ***Portuguese Trade with India in the sixteenth Century***, New Delhi (1983), pp. 237-38.
12. For Ayurvedic preparations herbs are weighed on the basis of Kazhanju.
13. Entrusting every thing to god/putting oneself in god's mercy.
14. Nakhuda-Nao (boat) + Khuda (Lord) = Lord of the Ship/Captain of the Ship.
15. Ship in which Ibn-Bettuta travelled to Calicut was owned by Nakhuda Mithqal (The founder of the Mithqal Masjid of Calicut but ship was leased by another Nakhuda.
16. As was done by Mughal Emperors for the purpose of Hajj pilgrims alone. Probably leased for the purpose.
17. Bari Sahiba, The Queen Mother of Bijapur in March 1663 bought a Gallion from the Portugues for Rs. 30,000 as she wanted go to Mecca. M. N Pearson in ***Studies in Maritime History***, p. 115.
18. There is an Arab proverb, 'When an Arab turns bankrupt, he looks for his father's papers' to find if there is any amount due from any one as payment to his father.

19. El-Khazaraji, ***History of Resuli Dynasty*** (ed) Muhammed Asal, (Leyden, 1906 to 1918) Vol. 4 p. 41.
20. lbn-Hadji, ***Al-Fatawa-Al-Kubra***, p. 26.
21. ***lbid.***, p. 115.
22. In Every pmt in Indian Ocean in Medieval time there was the office of Shahbandar. In Calicut the office was Shahbandar-Khwaja, more familiar in Malayalam as Sabantrakoya. The family is still in existence in Calicut.
23. Ibn Dajmar e. g., Speaks of a man who claimed he was the agent (Wakil) of Ahl Dabul people at Mocha.
24. S.D Goitein, ***Studies in Islamic History and Institution***, Leyden, (1966) 10-77.
25. Abdurahiman Khan-i-Khanan sponsored two ships for Hajj paying the full charge of the ship and expense of the passengers.
26. The Shaikh of Kazeruni was considered to be the patron saint of Mariners and had adherents all over trading world.
27. Sprencer Trimmingham, Sufi orders in Islam gives the working of large number of Khanqahs.
28. Dhikr (hymns) each Sufi order had its special Dhikar advised by the Shaikh which the Murid (Disciple) should always recite.
29. Short term, Contract marriages, there by finding a partner and house, which was welcome in all ports since the traders brought large fortunes.
30. 'Muwalladun' the name given to the Progency of Arab fathers and native women.
31. Even the words Seethi (sidi), Usthad, Muallim (Malumi) are such religious functionaries of maritime origin.
32. P. R. G. Mathur, ***The Mappila Fisher-Folk of Kerala***, Trivandrum 1978, pp, 304-313.

CHAPTER- IV

Maritime Allegories in Sufi Literature and Wall Paintings

As Muslims were generally familiar with ship and sea, maritime allegories were often used in Sufi works.

These works were mostly composed in flourishing centres of sea trade as early as 16th century. Hidayatul Adhkiya Ila Taiqatil Awliya, which is regarded as the manual of Sufism in Kerala by Shaikh Zainuddin Makkdum of Ponnani was completed in the year 1521. It has lines as follows:

> Who ever wish to get (obtain) Pearl (Haqiqah).[1] Let him embank the ship And on the ship later (You) get pearl (Realization of Ultimate truth)

The call is being made in the context of a Sufi's aspiration for attaining his object.

Philosophy–Kappappattu

Kappappattu/Ship song is a Sufi philosophical poem composed by Kunhayin Musliar, a learned scholar and courtier of Zamorin Rajas of Calicut and a close friend of Mangatt Achan, the Chief Minister of Zamorin. We have no exact information of his birth, but it is believed to be around 1700 AD. His poems have date of composition mentioned in all of them, and in some of them as chronograms.

His poem 'Nool Madhh' (Praise of thread) was composed in 1151 (H) on his longing and yearning of heart to meet Prophet Mohammed in life after death. The poem was written in 666 lines in 16 metres.

Ship song is his best philosophical poem where human body is compared with a ship, worldly life to the sailing of the ship, human mind to the captain of the ship and the port of destination of the ship to god (ultimate salvation).

A story is current about the reason for Kunhayin Musliyar composing the song. While undergoing his studies in Ponnani, the highest centre of Islamic learning in Malabar, he used to take his food from the home of his teacher Makhdum. Kunhayin Musliar was acclaimed as a great scholar and at the same time funny and witty. The wife of Makhdum once asked Kunhayin, what to recite while going to bed. "Elai Malai" said Kunhayin. The lady went on reciting the words. One day Mukhdum heared his wife reciting the words. He asked why do you recite these words, she said 'Kunhayin advised me'. Makhdum burst into laughter and exclaimed, "You still have not understood Kunhayin". The next day Makhdum asked Kunhayin "Are you making man a ship" while all the assembled laughed. After this incident, the author decided to write a ship song comparing man with ship.

The author writes that if the ship, human body has to reach safely without being obstructed by hazards at sea, the merchandise oftqwa (piety) should be loaded in it. He compared human limbs with different parts of the ship.

If the ship reaches safely its port of destination (Ultimate Salvation/ Paradise), the rewards waiting the ship (man) is described as follows.

Maidens will swing (you) in golden (swings)
Will eat fruits from great (good) trees
And good rivers to take and drink
Rivers of honey and milk
Rivers of wine flowing like a music
Young girls would come and bath (you)

And good spreaded beds
Then with handsome Prophet (Mohammed)
Help us Oh! God to witness those events
With Nabiulla, Tangal
Bless us to witness your 'Liqah' [2] gathering with your prophet help
us to witness
And bless me with death in 'Iman'[3]

Maritime similies had their influence even in paintings. At least one such group of paintings is present in one 18th century Mosque in Areacode of Malappuram district of Kerala. It is a riverine mosque. Such paintings though not common, would have existed, but not reported. The mosques in Kerala are always renovated and reconstructed and in places of mosques which were elegant examples of traditional architecture, concrete structures were erected, one sad impact of gulf money. Such is the case of the Jumaah Mosque of Chaliyam which was reconstructed in traditional style in 1573 with the materials returned to Muslims on the destruction of the Portuguese Fort of Chaliyam, by the Mappila-Zamorin alliances. But what we see now is a sterile concrete structure in its place and massive granite Cylindrical pillars which added grandeur to the structure, now lies scattered in the compound.

Fortunately in the Sunni mosque under discussion, no renovation had taken place. The mosque is still very spacious and the population increase did not affect it, because all the younger generation became Wahhabis and they constructed mosques in different parts of the town while the surroundings of the old mosque is used as graveyard by all groups of people.[4]

From the architectural features, it appears that the mosque is an eighteenth century construction. The massive wooden planks used as beams and lofty cylindrical columns, different from the traditional tapering wooden pillars of carpenters, the delicate carvings on doors and windows and the exquisitely decorated, Mirnber (Pulpit) are suggestive of its antiquity. The upper storey of the mosque is used for 'Dars'.[5]

Areacode is a riverine settlement on Chaliyar, some 20 miles east from its mouth 'Beypore'. C.A. Innes records that it was a confluence of highways of hill products and of important routes connecting Mysore.

The mosque is 100 mtrs away from the river on the way to erstwhile ferry from the main road. It is note worthy that in the absence of good roads, a feature noted by Europeans as late as 18th century[6], water transport was the main commercial miery of the country, especially of the interior to carry the products of the hinterlands, for floating down the therappam of timber and carrying back stapple food items like rice, sugar, dry fish and Tobacco etc. Hence rafts were on continuous move on these rivers as the cheapest means of transport. The town had an old quarter, now remnant of a centre of hectic commercial activity as the buildings would suggest, streets running parallel to the river and roads leading to the ferry. Such mosques were meant not only for the town people but also for sailors on the river.

This Muslim settlement is one of the links of the chain of Muslim settlement on Chaliyar River, beginning from Beypore, Feroke, Vazhakkard, Keezhuparambu, Ugrapuram, Areacode, Edavanna, Mampad and Futher east. Vazhakkad is one of the importent centres of Arabic learning. These centres developed as a consequence of Portuguese atrocities on Muslims in the port towns, when the later were compelled to move to the interior.[7]

The place name of the old quarter of the town 'Kufa' is also suggestive of its antiquity and of Sufi tradition. The residents of the area-majority of whom are averse to any Sufi tradition, due to the pre-dominance of Wahabis related to that, once an old man appeared in the street. He was followed and disturbed by boys. He then sarcastically remarked. "Oh, this is a Kufa itself', means a land of miscreants. But it seems that kufa is attached with a great sufi tradition. The best example of Sufis of Kufa is Shaykh Aliyyul Kufi, who settled in Peringathur village of Kozhikode in 16th century, developing that area to a Muslim centre.[8]

A Qabar attached to the front wall of the mosque is seen with an iron lamp and lighted wicks. People could be seen offering prayers.[9]

Old men related that it was the Qabar of the holy man instrumental in constructing the mosque.[10]

On the wall of the mosque, eight paintings are now seen though some have been erased. One of them is a calligraphy work, and another is a square table of 16 columns in which the physical features of prophet is artistically written. Another table is a popular poem in Arabi-Malayalam describing the method of deciding the time of prayers measuring one's own shadow in different months.[11]

Masjidul Haram (Mecca) is painted on top of one of the entrances signifying a believers entry to that sacred shrine when a Muslim enters that Masjid. The position of Kaba, the line of ***Tawaf*** (circumambulation) the position of entrance, names of 'Bab' (door), the light points are all clearly marked. Another painting is of Madeena Munawwara (The mosque of prophet). We have every reason to believe that this is a depiction by one who had seen it, by a Haji.

Paintings of two ships are most important of the group. One of them unfinished appears to be of later date. But portrait of an elegant ship, so live as if moving on the sea with fullspread sails and fluttering flags is the most attractive work here. The descriptive notes are given in Arabic and Arabi-Malayalam. Many phrases used are typical of very old usage of Mappila (Muslim) Malayalalm. It reads: This ship (Islam) has five 'Komb' (Mast) representing five pillars of Islam.

1. The mast of ***Shahadat***
2. The mast of ***Salath*** (5 times prayer)
3. The mast of ***Zakath*** (poor right)
4. The mast of ***Ramzan*** (fast)
5. The mast of ***Hajj.***

As the six canons of Iman (Belief) the ship is six storied, and each story is drawn giving full description of man.

The five masts have sails according to shipping rules. The first mast have a small sail (top) and two big ones. These two sails on the mast of '***Shahadat***' represents

1. No god except Allah and
2. Mohammed is his Messenger

The second mast of prayer has 5 sails representing 5 times prayer. To climb up the mast pole where sails begin, two ladders are provided as Ladder of '***Shart***' (condition for prayer). The steps of ladder (5) are described as follows:

1. To know the Waqt-Time of prayer
2. Ablution
3. Keep the body clean
4. Cover the '***awrath***' (such parts of the body that must be covered)
5. Facing Qibla

The third mast, of fast has 3 sails representing

1. The first ten fast
2. The second ten
3. The third ten

and the topmost (small) sail representing the fast of '***Ashura***'. The fourth mast of ***Zakkat***. The fifth mast of ***Hajj*** has five sails representing five important ceremonies of ***Hajj***. A ladder to reach the bottom (beginning) of the sail represents '***Aavathu***' (capability) to perform ***Hajj***.

The sail represents the ceremonies in order.

1. Sail of 'Ihram'[12] of Meeqat[13]
2. Stay in Arafa[14]
3. Thawaf[15]
4. Saiyu[16] (Run)
5. Cutting hair.[17]

An old cast type canon is seen fixed in front (***Aniyam***) and it is written, "The fire is on 'Iblis', Satan".

The sukkan of ***Aql*** (Rudder of wisdom) is significant. The connecting pulleys, the ***Alaths*** (ropes) and even the fluttering flag on the ropes have been rendered to represent important cardinals of Islam.

The painter envisaged it a big ship representing life and evils of life are represented as thieves, four in number.

1. ***Iblis***–Satan
2. ***Duniya***–world
3. ***Jasad***– body
4. Men

All the four causing trouble in a life of piety which Islam (the ship) should adopt. Even the lights hung on the topmost ropes connecting the top of masts have been given befitting names. The first of the light being the night of ***Qadr***.[18] The second is lamp of 'Id' and the third is light of 'Bakrid'. The three lights giving light to the ship is representing tlu·ee festive occasions, shedding light in a believer's life. A fascinating allegory indeed.

A small life boat of '***Ilm***' (knowledge) is tugged to the ship, its size compared to the ship shows that the painter envisaged the whole theme as a perfect ship. The harmonious combination of even the minute details of sail and ship is a replica of the religion of Islam as he understood. The whole painting is very lively. The fluttering flags and full spread curved sails give the impression of a smooth sailing ship on a high sea.

It seems that the painter was a deep scholar and a sailor with vast experience of ship and sea with acquaintance of the sacred shrines.

The work was probably undertook as a vow as it includes all tenets of Islam, ship and Kaaba.

The mosques are loosing their historical materials as the traditional buildings with exquisite architectural beauty, are being pulled down to raise concrete structures, enabled by gulf money. A glaring example was the demolition of Mamburam mosque which proudly bore the marks of police firing, sparking the 1921 rebellion. Another example was the masjid of Edavanna, where the massive lotus shaped wooden pillars supported the first floor with embossed wood carvings of ***Quran*** on the bottom of all the wooden frames.

This painting is glowing tribute to the life of a medieval sailor who was a good navigator and knew the nook and corner of the ship and sailing. He was a well versed scholar of religion and theology, because the discussion overboard all along the journey was bound to be religious. A mariner had to be an expert manager of finance and above all he could speak many languages especially of all the ports his ship often called at.

This painting of ship combined with religious principle meant for a society which could understand and appreciate the overall theme of the work, which is another example of maritime traditions in Muslim life and painting.

Reference

1. The ultimate longing of a sufi to get Haqiqah (The reality, ultimate truth, Creator).
2. 'Liqah' meeting. The most graceful thing in life after death is 'meeting' the 'Lord' as Muslims believe for good people and sinners will be denied the privilege of meeting Lord.
3. C.N. and K.K.M.A. Karim (Op. Cit), p. 168.
4. Information gathered from field study and enquiries on the spot.
5. The place where the pupil undergoing teaching and training of Aiim is conducted.
6. Small principalities of the chieftains, the boundaries were often rivers with steep banks often subjected to floods caused roads impracticable without bridges which required huge investment. Moreover income frame ferries formed an important income of local Rajas. Even the joint commissioners later reported the pitiable condition of roads in Malabar.
7. Inhuman Portuguese atrocities on Muslim population compelled them to move to the interior, along the rivers, the regions with which they were more conversant, and riverine settlements sprang up. The traditional agrarian society of Malabar had stress and strains to accommodate the newcomers in the community modeled on caste, land and land rights. Muslims lost monopoly of high sea trade, and became petty shopkeepers, brokers and landless labourers. And people began to walk by hillocks (leaving plains). Qazi Mohammed, Fathhul Mubin. (R.E. Miller, ***Mappila Muslims of Kerala-Madras*** (1976), pp. 75.)
8. The date of Aliyyul Kufi's life and works is understood from the 'Manaqib' (hagiographic Literature–Songs, etc.) of another very popular saint of Porathel in Kannur district, Abdul Qadir Sani of Suhrawandi Silsila. He styled himself as Abdul Qadir Sani, (Second Abdul Qadir) out of respect for Shaykh Abdul Qadir Jilani, the Universal Saint. It says that Abdul Qadir had visited Aliyyul Kufi in his cave hermitage in Kanakamala. A chronogram in Arabic proves his date in 16th century (d983 AH)
9. These practices are now discarded as ***Kufr*** (Disbelief) and ***Shirk*** (Idolatry)
10. The storey is as follows: One Raja of Nilambur Kovilakam fell seriously ill under an incurable disease. A Muslim Faqir cured him. The Raja who was very much pleased gave him land to erect a mosque. After his death he was buried close to the foundation of the mosque.

11. These poems were memorised by all in the days when there was no clocks, loudspeakers or ***Nakharas*** (Kettledrums).
12. A man in his consciousness confirms the 'intention' to perform ***Hajj***.
13. A point at a specific distance from the holy house where a man starts the ceremonies of ***Hajj***.
14. The places of assembly where all Muslims performing ***Hajj*** should assemble and spend part of night, where prophet Mohammed made his farewell speech.
15. Circumambulation of Kaba in anti-clock wise.
16. Running between the two points Safa and Marva.
17. The last rite of Hajj.
18. The 27th night of Ramzan the most auspicious day for Muslim when Quran was first revealed to prophet Mohammed.

CHAPTER-V

The Marakkar Legacy and Mappila Community

The general acceptance of the ideals of ***Shahid*** (Martyr) and the consequent growth of militancy was the Mappila response to Portuguese atrocities on Malabar and its people.

The Portuguese, for the first time introduced use of force in trade in Indian Ocean. When the Arabs took over the monopoly of spice trade from Romans, almost simultaneously the religion of Islam was established as the most powerful political force of the world. The founding of Baghdad, the change of course of Eastern merchandise from trans-Arabian routes to Euphrates Tigris river systems and the growth of Abbasid Caliphate added the prestige and increased the profit of traders.[1]

The Pax-Islamica of four centuries (800-1200) gave a boost to the commerce and the Caliphal Empire itself became a vast consumer market, again increasing the profit.

A large share of the profit of spice trade went as ***Zakath*** to common people, as offerings to the pious holymen and shrines, a still larger sum was distributed. The ***Khanqahs*** and ***Darghas*** of Patron Saints[2] of Mariner people and often individual contributions and personal endowments were of great help for the development of Muslim settlements all over the Indian Ocean Lithoral.

It was this flourishing trade that the Portuguese usurped with force and brutality. A direct fight with the Portuguese was impossible since they had superior fire arms, which Muslim traders and natives rulers had not tried to develop, as it was not considered necessary in a peaceful trade.[3] The Portuguese captured Arab Traders, burnt ***hajj*** ships destroyed mosques, reviled Prophet Mohammed, dugout***Qabars*** and desecrated Quran.[4] It was at this juncture of political and social developments that the theologians of Ponnani preached a ***Jihad*** (holy war) binding on every Muslim. Shaikh Zainuddin Makhdum of Ponnani in ***Tuhfat ul Mujahidin*** regarded the arrival of Portuguese as a punishment of God since the Muslims of Malabar went astray from the true religion.[5] In ***Tuhfa***t he explained the reward and bliss of martyrdom and the elevated status of ***shahid*** on the day of Judgement. Even before ***Tuhfat***, a work of similar nature with same purpose–***A Qasid***a–long poem in Arabic–***Tahrid Ahl il Iman Ala Jihadi Abdathissulban***[6] was written. Abdathissulban means worshippers of cross. This notion to fight the worshippers of cross takes its origin from the crusades and Christian- Muslim conflict on the Iberian peninsula, ending the Muslim rule in Spain. This call made from Ponnani spread all over Mappila land since it was in Ponnani that the theologians called Musaliyars were trained.

Adbutha Ratna Mala or ***Kottuppalli Mala***, a very popular hagiographic composition also greatly influenced the people. He Here Manath Veetil Kunhi Marakkar goes out of his maninage pavellion to rescue a Muslim girl, captured by the Portuguese, from a ship anchored off the shore. In the mid-night he rescued the girl, but himself was killed and his body was cut into pieces. Several pieces were washed ashore and they were buried. Later miracles occurred in places where his limbs were buried. The tradition of human limbs appearing, their burials and miracles were so appealing to the public that later on there arose traditions of mutilated human limbs appearing even in interior places far off from seashore.

It was in this tradition of militancy and martyrdom that Kunhali Marakkars arose. There were four of them in the illustrious line. Kunhali Marakkars (1507-31), II (1531-71), III (1571-95), IV (1595-99). We hear of the first Marakkar in history of Malabar in 1502 when the Raja of Cochin befriended the Portuguese and Cochin became just another port like Lisboa. Ismail Marakkar, the head of rice-merchants from Konkan, protested prohibiting his fellow traders importing of rice to Cochin.

The Marakkars then moved to a safer place to Ponnani. The Portuguese bombarded Ponnani as it was Naval base of Zamorin and Marakkars moved to Calicut[7] and still north to Pantalayini.

The origin of the name Marakkar has been discussed in detail by many historians. The word originated from Maram or Kattamaram, the earliest form of boat. The owner of a boat is called Marakkan. When a honorific plural 'r' is given it becomes Marakkav. Origin of the word 'Kunhali Marakkav' has also been discussed widely. According to the present writer, the word is Kunha + Ali + Marakkar. Kunha (beloved, younger) in Zamorin's hierarchy of nobility was a honorific title reserved for persons very close to the Raja, or members of the Royal family like Kunhunni Raja or Kunhanuj an Raja or Elaya or Mutha etc. Ali the fourth Caliph of Islam, the son-in-law of Prophet Mohammed in medieval times (in Islamic traditions) was a synonym of valour, courage and bravery and was called ***Asad*** (Lion–Arabic), ***Sher*** (Lion in Persian and Urdu) and ***Puli*** (Tiger) in Malayalam). Thus Ali was specific title for Naval commanders. Other Naval commanders of the day e.g. the Turkish commander sent by Pasha to India to oppose the Portuguese had the title ***'Sidi Ali Reis'***. Again Ibn Majid who steered Vasco da Gama's ship from Melindi to Calicut, had the surname 'Asadul Bahr·' which J.R. Tibbet has translated as 'Lion of the Sea'. Kunhali Marakkar thus would mean 'closest (to the Raja) Admiral Lion of the Sea'. Such title had great significance. While the Navy of Bijapur, Gujarat, Egypt and Turkey were fighting the Portuguese, a man of very high rank had to be the Naval commander of Zamorin, who was in fact to co-ordinated the Naval wars.

How could the Maraldcars fight so daringly against the Portuguese Galleys mounted with heavy canons with their swords and small boats called Paraohs is a baffling question. It seems that Marakkar fighters were recruited as members of a Sufi brotherhood sworn to fight unto death. This is clear from the two ***Qabars*** on the western side of Mihrab and pulpit of Kunhali Marakkar's Masjid in his old capital of Puthuppanam Fort. They are covered with green silks and an offering box is kept nearby. There is a tradition in the construction of Masjids in Malabar that the man who was instrumental in building of Masjid will be buried near the walls, on the eastern side of the masjid. In this case, the ***Qabar*** being on the western side, this was intentionally put there since all those who perform prayers in the Mosque do obeisance to these ***Qabars***. The Sufi order was probably Qalandar sect, the evidence being discussed in a different context in this work. The Marakkar fighters, all had shaven heads, without shirts wearing typical clothes, Belts and Talismans with red scarfs as the large paintings now exhibited in the Goan Museum show with the note Malabares killing Portuguese Padres?[8] The Malabares are obviously Marakkar soldiers.

Kunhali Marakkar IV took over as the chief of Puthuppanam Kotta in 1595 after the death of Pattu Marakkar, third Kunhali Marakkar and the founder of the Kotta. The strong fort and consolidation of his navy convinced the Portuguese of the need of destroying him and his fort. The Portuguese were trying systematically to cause a wedge between Zamorin and his Naval Commander. Even his predecessor had began to feel of such a tactics and the joint authors of Saga of Kunhalis noted Kunhali IIIrd died with a heavy heart filled with the gloomy prospects of the end of all the great work, the illustratious Marakkars had done for the zamorins.[9] It is also said that his power and victories had swelled his head and Kunhali Marakkar had taken titles Amirul Muminin[10] and protector of Islam etc. The conspiracy finally hatched.

Zamorin invested the fort from land and the Portuguese from the sea. Many Portuguese commanders were routed and finally Andre Furtado, the grandson of Vasco-da Gama took charge of the siege. The heroic resistance of Marakkar or the efficient leadership of Furtado is not the theme of discussion here. Marakkar surrendered to Zamorin and was caught un-armed by Furtado and carried away to Portuguese quarters. The tumult caused in Zamorin's Nair soldiers had to be pacified by allowing them to ransack the fort. Kunhali Marakkar was taken to Goa with 40 prisoners. A rift and jealousy formed between

Governor Menzes of Goa and Furtado, over claiming the credit of capturing the dreaded enemy of the Portuguese. The whole people of Goa and Lisbon celebrated it. Marakkar was killed with a specially constructed scaffold. His body was quartered and exhibited on the beach of Panjim and Bardez, head was salted and sent to Cannanore to strike terror among the Mappilas. The death of Kunhali marked the end of a glorious chapter in the history of India and inaugurated the end of Zamorin's rule as O.K. Nambiar observed. But it was not the end of Kunhali Marakkar legacy.

Though Kunhali IV was no more, it appears as if he was reborn.[11] A cousin of Kunhali IV, who was at the age of 13 captured by Furtado and brought to Goa was baptised and later married to a Portuguese orphan. He was given the christian name of Pedor Rodrigues. Pyrard de Laval, the French traveller had seen him working in one of the Portuguese galleys. He had witnessed the fate of Kunhali IV. One night he secretly fled from Goa and managed to reach Malabar safely. He collected the Marakkar fighters with 5 Paraos and started harassing the Portuguese relentlessly and looted their ships frequently. He went down to Cape Comorin and to the north-west province of Ceylon and from there to the Island of Tandiva. There he entered the beach of St. Joao and took revenge on the Franciscan priests for the baptism, he had received from them at Goa years before. This act of Pedro Rodrigues clearly shows that though a Christian for over 20 years, he had hated the Portuguese and went on robbing and plundering the Portuguese ships, where ever it was possible. The menace was so great that the king of Pmiugal had instructed the Viceroy of Goa that all the vessels should sail heavily armed and must be convoyed.

A series of letters from March to June 1619, from Constantino Desa of Ceylon to Viceroy's Council, show how terribly shaken the Portuguese administration in Ceylon was due to Pedro's destruction, who had seized the Fort of Ilhas das Vacas.[12]. He threatened Coromondal coast and caused great damage to Portuguese trade. On 27 November 1619, in an engagement with Victoria da Abreau, Pedro captured 12 out of 18 ships, killed 300 men in action and enslaved the rest including Victoria da Abreau himself. Both Pedro's booty and prestige were at that time greater than any of his predecessors.

With the exit of Portiuguese from the scene the Dutch depredations on the Malabar coast increased. In a desperate attempt to save his interest the Zamorin tried to revive the Marakkars.

The investiture ceremony of Kunhali Marakkars in the Calicut Grandhavari of 1667 discovered by Dr. N.M. Namboothiri was such an attempt of Zamorin. The non-cooperation of 'Malabares' had diminished pepper trade and Francise da Costa entirely omitted Calicut from his detailed account of pepper trade of the day a sure indication of its insignificance as an official source of supply of pepper for the Portuguese.

The Grandhavari shows that for the investiture ceremony, 500 panams (quarter rupee) were spent[13] a fairly large amount coming up to Rs. 80000/- present. This record has the word ***Qalandar***[14] indicating Sufi affiliation of Marakkars.

Following the occupation of Malabar by the English after 1799, there arose the Mappila outbreaks of 19th century (1851-1921) fifty-one in all. Since only 28 out of 350 who directly participated in 51 outbreaks returned, it becomes clear that the intentional martyrdm was their special characteristic. The basic cause of the outbreaks, which William Logan assessed as agrarian unrest again proves the community's readiness to fight unto death against any injustice, which their leaders perceived as an attack on the community. The last of the series of the outbreaks was in 1921.

During 1921 we find readiness of the conununity to fight. The emotional issue of Khilafat movement, influence of Congress and Nationalism and the grievances of Kudiyan Sangham had sparked the agitation.

All along the course of the history of Mappila community, we find the Marakkar legacy of Martyrdom in a Sufi brotherhood.

We find confiscated Preachers' handbooks authored by eminent theologians and preachers, calling people to fight a holy war against Britishers to protect Osmanli Khilafat/Unite under him to fight the enemies of the Caliph and to expel the non-Muslim from Arab sacred land and the two sacred cities compulsory on every Muslim as farcl Aine.[15]

The talisman worn by Marakkar fighters (of Qalandriya sect) and the talisman of Mamburam Tangal worn by Mappilas in 1921, to protect from police fire were identical symbols of the intentional martyrdom and Sufi legacy of the community.

Origin of Kunhali Marakkars and Organization of their Fighters

As Naval chieftains of the Zamorins, Kunhali Maraldcars are familiar to students of history. Works on Kerala history refer to the Zamorin's appointment of Kunhali Marakkars as his captains. The following casual statements remain unexplained. How the Marakkars originated? Where did they come from? How did they organize themselves to fight to death? What was their social and economic status? Again what was their position in the hierarchy? These are baffling questions to a modern researcher.

Marakkars emerged as a decisive factor in the history of Kerala in the Zamorin's battle against the Raja of Cochin. When the Raja of Cochin befriended the Portuguese to defeat the Zamorin with the help of the new sea-power, the Zamorin realized the threat to his sea-trade and pre- eminence of Calicut on the west coast, and induced by his Muslim subjects-the main target of Portuguese brunt- besieged Cochin in 1503.[16]

On the Zamorin's inducement, Ismail Marakkar issued orders prohibiting the trade in rice with Cochin. [17] This shows that Marakkar community were traders in rice from Konkan.

In Calicut also, rice was imported by Muslim traders. When Vasco da Gama was off Calicut during his second atTival, he had fallen upon a t1otilla of twenty-four Calicut boats with a crew of 800, all laden with rice from Konkan. The cruelties[18] that perpetuated on the members of the rice-importing community was a warning to the community in Cochin too. In medieval times, trading communities had definite sphere of operation and had specialized commodities. The Muslim's business community of Cochin was composed of the Marakkars importing rice and Ismail Marakkar who headed the trading community was a rich merchant, probably with privileges like

Sabantra Koya (Shahbandar Khwaja) of Calicut, or with immense wealth as Nakhuda Mithqal whom Ibn Battuta has so well described.

The Raja of Cochin entered into a treaty of friendship with Portuguese and "Cochin became another Portuguese town like Lisbon". This might have hampered the trading activities of Muslims and the Marakkar community moved to the Mappila centre of Ponnani in search of a free port. Ponnani, the arsenal and naval headquarters of Zamorin was soon to become the Portuguese target for destruction. Due to constant bombardment of the town, the Marakkars of Ponnani again moved to north and finally took up the Naval Captainship of the Zamorins.

It seems that Marakkars had earlier settlements north of Calicut also.[19] The Zamorin, after destruction of the Chaliyam fort in 1573, granted permission to Pattu Marakkar–who led the attack on the fort– to erect a fort with all honours of a Nayar chieftain, and title Kunhali (the third). Why Puthuppanam was selected for the fort then? It is quite possible that Puthuppanam had been one of the Marakkar settlements, with Pantalayani Kollam nearby. Logan observes that, it was after the attack of Henry Menezes in 1525 on Pantalayani Kollam, which was a stronghold of Kunhalis (Marakkars), and on Ponnani, where he destroyed several Moorish ships, that the Maraldcars appeared as the spearhead of the Mappila resistance.

There were powerful Marakkar settlements on the east coast and in some cases their own fortifications such as Kotta in Ceylon. Their successful operation from Gujarat to the straits would not have been possible, had it not been for local support.[20]

Thus, Marakkars were a powerful trading community of rich merchants by the time when Zamorin was looking for allies to repel the Portuguese. Even before the Zamorin-Marakkar alliance , 'Mercantile battles' had been fought in the Arabia Sea.

The origin of the word Marakkar is traced to an Arabic root Markab, in an attempt to find an Arabic origin for every name as Labbai or Nawayats. The name is also traced to the Tunisian word Martaba[21] (sailor). It is a common feature that all the maritime communities of coastal settlements try to trace their origin to the oppressive rule of Hajjaj bin Yusuf (692-718), the Umayyad Governor, the consequent migration and hence an Arabic origin for their names. The Marakkar tradition is that when the first immigrants of this class landed on Indian shores, they were naturally asked who they were and whence they came. In answer, they pointed to their boats and pronounced the word Markab, and in consequence they became known to the Hindus as Marakkayar or people from Markab. There are many objections to accepting this story.

A more reasonable suggestion is that since they originated in the eastern coast, roots of the name are to be sought there. It seems that the word originated from Cattamaram or Maram which means a raft or boat. The owner of a Maram is called Marakkan.

The fishermen folk in general is called Marakkan, as we see in Thakazhi's Chemmeen where the fisher woman calls her husband Marakkan. If, simply, the plural or an honorific 'r' is added, marakkan becomes Marakkar. This assumption is supported by Madras census report of 1901, where Marakkars are describe as "a Tamil-speaking Mussalman tribe of mixed Hindu and Mussalman origin, the people of which are usually traders. In the Gazetteer of South Arcot district, the Marakkayars are described as "Largely big Traders with other countries such as Ceylon and strait settlements and owning most of the native coasting crafts."[22] "Owning most of the coasting craft" is again a proof of large population.

A palm leaf manuscript of 1667 in the Calicut Grandhavari[23] has the name 'Marakkayar', which undoubtedly proves that the origin of the name is from 'Maram' as its respective plural of 'Maraldcayar'.

The above manuscript also confirms a mystique organization of Marakkars/fighters. As the last Kunhali (the fourth) was hanged in Goa and the Marakkar fighters were no more allies of the Zamorins, the Dutch could constantly ransack Zamorin's ports. There had been an increase in the frequency of attacks on the southern ports in the middle of 17th century.

This compelled the Zamorin to revive Marakkar fighters and conferment of title of 1667 referred in the Grandhavari was an attempt to placate these fighters. The palm leaf Manuscript reads.[24]

"After the casket and green silk was offered as tribute and after he did obeisance as in olden days for the said Kunhi Qalandar (conferred) the title of Marakkayar with power of a chieftain. And (by) Ittinarayana Nambi the lamp was also given (Right to lighten day lamp in Kunhali's entourage).

Dr. N.M. Namboothiri unfortunately mistook 'Qalandar' as Commander. He could not comprehend the intricacies of the Ghazi tradition of medieval times, an Islamic counter-part of crusader. Such titles have been accepted even by rulers and men had been initiated to such groups with elaborate ritual ceremonies.

'Qalander' is a kind of itinerating Muhammadan Monk with shaven head and beard, who abandons everything–wife, friends, possessions and wanders in the world[25] . A Qalandar was member of Qalandariya sect, 'A sect of Muhammadan Dervishes pledged to perpetual wandering'.[26] A field study conducted in Irinjalkotta (old fortress of Kunhali Marakkars) confirmed this mystic tradition. The central mosque of Marakkars in the old fortress still exists with Mimber (pulpit), where a beautiful gold painted carved wooden plank is mounted, which Kunhali had once captured from the Portuguese. There is a tradition in the medieval mosques in Kerala, that either the founder of the mosque or a holy man who was instrumental in the construction of the mosque will be buried very close or nearby the foundation of the mosque. In the Iringal Masjid, two Qabars (Tombs) of 'Sufis' are seen with offering box and covered with green silk. These were probably the tombs of spiritual mentors of Kunhalis.

The residents, descendants of the Marakkar family informed that till some twenty years ago, a man lived there with a coat and cap who was popularly known as Qalandar.

We know that Kunhalis and their fighting men were called pirates by the Portuguese who considered themselves as legitimate heirs of seaborne trade. In the St. Francis Convent Museum under the A.S.I. in Goa, dozens of paintings are preserved, all showing the 'Malabarese killing St. Franciscan padres'. These Malabarese are Kunhalis and their fighters–all with shaven heads and beards with a silk turban, all without shirts. This seems to be the prescribed dress of the Qalandar brotherhood of Kunhalis and their fighters[27].

Hence, it is right to assume that the Zamorin allied himself with this powerful mercantile community to oppose the Portuguese and conferred on them the title 'Kunhali'. As Miller pointed out, when the pet name Kunha (younger, beloved) is added to Ali, the word Kunhali would mean Dear Ali or younger Ali, and when added Marakkar it means Dear Ali the Navigator, or Sir Ali the Navigator.[28]

Here a more meaningful suggestion could be made. The Zamorin had appointed Kunhali Marakkar as his captain, conferring upon him all the powers of a Nayar Cheiftain with the right to wear a silk turban. The title Kunha means younger or '***Elaya***'. ***Elaya*** and ***Mutha*** (Elder) had been some of the titles of the feudatories and Naduvalis of the Zamorins who were called for Ariyittuvalcha (Coronation). In K.V. Krishna Ayyar's ***The Zamorins of Calicut***, we come across a long list of such names. Some of the are-[29]:

1. Chemmanikkara Mutha Nayar,
2. Valayur Mutha Eradi,
3. Palayancheri Valuthaya Nayar,
4. Mulanchur Elaya Nayar,
5. Tinayancheri Elayath, and
6. Parachattam Patanayar.

Since '***Elaya***' and '***Mutha***' were positional titles of the Zamorin's nobles, Kunha also probably had been a positional title. It can be an office of status and authority in the hierarchy. The Zamorin's Act of permitting Pattumarakar with the title of Kunhali Maraldcar–to erect a fort at Puthuppanam, etc. may be viewed in this context, in the context of nobility and not a mere title conferred as of recognition of his services.

While Egyptian, Gujarat and Bijapur rulers led the opposition to the Portuguese, in Calicut the anti-Portuguese operation was led by one important feudatory of the Zamorins. Kunhali Marakkar, therefore, means Elaya Ali, the Navigator. As Patanayar is the head of the Zamorin's Army, Maraldcar was chief of the Navy and therefore Kunhali Marakkar would mean Elaya Ali, the Admiral or Admiral Elaya Ali with all powers and privileges of a Nayar chieftain who was designated as 'Elaya'.

The position of Kunhali Maraldcar in the Zamorin's nobility can be understood from the fact that for their investiture ceremony 500 'panams' (a quarter rupee) were spent, a fairly large amount coming upto roughly Rs. 80,000.[30] The non-cooperation of 'Malabarese' had practically diminished pepper trade and Francise da Costa, entirely omitted Calicut from his detailed account of Malabar pepper trade- A sure indication of its insignificance as an official source of supply for the Portuguese.[31] The Zamorin's attempts to befriend Maraldcars is to be seen in this context.

Further 'Kunha' was the honorific title reserved only for the members of the Royal family.

Reference

1. The Arab geographers mention five important kings in the world, the first being the Abbasid Caliph himself.
2. Mariner people of all nations and age had patron saints. In medieval times the Shaikh of Kazerun in Persia was regarded as patron saint of Mariners in eastern waters. There had been Kazeruni Khanqahs (hospices) all over trading world. In Calicut there had been one such Khanqah. Ibn-Batuta mentions that 300 students in the Mosque of Pantalayini Kgllam were maintained with the contribution of shipowners and traders who called on the Port.
3. Barbossa says while Vasco-da Gama fired Canons on city of Calicut, Zamorin's people retaliated but their shots came like pebbles".
4. The description of Portuguese atrocities is available in Fathhul Mubin of Quazi Mohammed (1573) also Tuhfat....
5. Shaikh Zainuddin regarded the arrival of Portuguese as a Punishment of God to Muslims of Malabar.
6. Inducement to fight the Worshippers of cross. (Unpublished).
7. "In the same year (1524) some of the Faquirs of Koshi (Cochin) like Ahamad Marakkar his brother Kunjali Marakkar, their uncle Muhammed Ali Marakkar and other dependents felt heir desire to wage war against the Portuguese they left Koshi for Kalikut, Zainuddin, ***Tuhfat***, p. 5.
8. These large paintings were originally kept in Viceroy's Palace and now in Museum near Bom Jesus Church, Goa.
9. Dr. K.K.N. Kurup and Dr. K.M. Mathew (Ed) ***Native Resistance Against the Portuguese***, Calicut (2000), p. 16.
10. Commander of Believers a title which the Caliphs used to take pride.
11. Dr. K.K.N. Kurup and Dr. K.M. Matlwe (Ed.) ***op.cit.***, p. 102.
12. ***Ibid.***, p. 103.
13. Calculated from the price equivalent of pepper of same quantity.

14. Unfortunately Dr. N.M. Namboothiri translated Qalandar as commander.
15. Aminummantakatb Pareekutty Musliar, Muhimmathul Muminin (Ar) unpublished.
16. K.M. Panikkar, ***A History of Kerala***, 1498-1801 (1960), p. 57.
17. Cochin was a rice-deficit area as was Calicut. Rice was importe from Canara Coast.
18. He (Vasco da Gama) ordered his men to cut off their hands and ears. This done, their feet were tied together, and in order to prevent them from untying the cords with teeth, he ordered his men to strike them on their mouths with staves and knock their teeth down their throat. They were then put on board, heaped one up on top of the other and covered with mats and dry leaves; the sails were then set for the shore and the vessels set on fire. Danvers, F.C. ***The Portuguese in India*** (London, 1894), p. 5.
19. Around 1540 we hear of Mammali Marakkar who was the richest merchant in Cannanore. Murder of his cousin Abubakr Ali by the Portuguese was one of the causes of the breach of Zamorin-Portuguse Treaty of 1540. R.R.S. Chauhan in Dr. Teutonio R.D' Souza (ed), ***Essays on Goan History***, pp. 30-31.
20. After the destruction of Kunhali Marakkars we find one member of the family organizing Marakkar supporters and fighting the Portuguese. R.R.S. Chauhan, ***pp.Cit.***, pp. 35-37.
21. P.K. Muhammad Kunhi, ***Muslimkalum Kerala Charithrauvm*** (Mal.) (Tricur, 1982), p. 92.
22. E. Thurston, ***Castes and Tribes of Southern India***, Vol. V, p. l.
23. No. 16, p. 33A in possession of Dr. N.M. Namboothiri has reference to the investitutre of Kunhali Marakkar.
25. N.M. Namboothiri, ***Samoothiri Charithrathinte Kanappurangal*** (Mal.) (Unseen pages of Zamorin's history), 1987, pp. 16, 286.
25. F. Steingass, ***Persian-English Dictionary*** (Delhi, 1973), p. 986.
26. ***Ibid.***
27. Mr. K.K. Muhammed, Dy. Superintending Archaeologist of the Goa Circle had been kind enough to let me inspect many dozens of preserved and unpreserved paintings in the store of the Museum, all collected from the Viceroy's Palace after the liberation of Goa, which was 'Se Cathedral' the biggest church in Asia when it was constructed in the site of the destroyed Adilshahi palace.
28. R.E. Miller, ***Mappila Muslims of Kerala***, p. 68.
29. K.V. Krishna Ayyar, ***The Zamorins of Calicut***, (Calicut, 1938), pp. 325-27. Appendix Ill- Feudatories and Naduvalis etc. invited for Ariyittuvalcha.
30. A letter from Crisna Annavy (11 Nov. 1746) directing Angengo factory to purchase pepper at Rs. 65/- candy was taken as a base for calculation. Equivalent price of candy (about 560 pounds) was calculated giving due allowance to the time lag between 1667-1746. This letter is referred in A. Das Gupta, ***Malabar in Asian Trade***, 1740-1840 (Cambridge, 1967),p. 37.
31. A.R. Disney, ***Harward Historical Studies–Twilight of the Pepper Empire***, (Harward, 1978), p. l81.

CHAPTER-VI

Working Groups Life Onboard and Rituals

Construction of a ship is carried as a solemn rite by workers in all stages, as they believe it acquires life with the final rite of opening the eye' (Kannu Thurakkal). Work in the building yards begin with construction of a large pavellion, sufficient to accommodate the ship till the work is completed. The work may also begin without the pavellion being constructed in advance, if the rainy season is not near. As the building yards on the river side are thickly covered with tall cocoanut trees, they would shelter from direct sun. A pavellion is necessary because it may take 1, 1.5 , 2 or 2.5 years to complete one vessel, without leave other than weekly and festival holidays.

The silence and discipline during the work other than the notice of carpenters at work or of a drill, can be witnessed in the yard. They enter the ship only barefooted.

Boat building traditions are intimately associated with religious beliefs and superstitious. Every major phase of the activity–felling trees, laying keel fixing mast–is associated with rituals.[1]

The work begins with ***Bhoomipooja*** performed by a Brahmin. After the ***pooja,*** a Moulavi or Tangal (Sayyid) offers '***Dua***' (prayer) and animal sacrifice is followed. Some times goats are sacrificed at both ends of the keel. Generally the owner from far off gulf country, the owner of the shipyard, the agent, Mestri and all workers would be present on the occasion.

Sathyan, the Mestri of the largest ship now being built[2] in Beypore told me that it may take 2.5 years and 15000 labour days to complete the work. Yet only the body, 50% of the work will be completed in the yard, then it is tugged to the gulf and interior decoration as a tourist boat will be done there. It seems that Beypore is regaining its past glory. The ship is ordered for Sheikh Ahamed bin Khalifa al thani of the Qatar Royal family.

The keel of this ship is 145 ft which is joined in tongue and grove method, which has won the praise of European travellers especially Varthema and Barbossa. It is a heavy block.

Measuring 16" x 18", strongest wood formerly it was Karmaruthu, now an equivalent of the same Malaysian wood. The planks are essentially teak but Burmese teak.

The Odayis are now spread in Beypore, Feroke, Chaliyam and Mannoor regions. They are divided into three categories A, B and C, and are paid according to experience, workout put and expertise as follows:

A = 800
B = 700
C = 650-600

The chief Odayisreceives the amount and distributes it. He said the same was the old age practice in the field. It is insisted that, Odayis should be free from vices like drinking so that mind and thought should be clear. A little carelessness will undo the entire work. The European writers have us believe that Indian ships were Sewen, and did not use iron nails. But the presence of a settlement called 'Karuvanthuruthi' (Settlement of Black smiths) proves that Blacksmiths were in need in Beypore. In no other place, a 'settlement' of Blacksmiths existed. The iron parts are now being manufactured outside. On the two ends of the pandi (keel), thathila are fixed for ***Aniyam*** (front) and ***Amaram*** (rear). Then the ***kalu*** (ribs) are fixed on which the planks are fixed with nails.[3] At bottom of the thathila of ***Aniyam*** (rear), an arch shaped space is created where the fan of the engine is to be fitted. This arch construction is called '***korwan***'. This ship has a unique addition, a middle structure in the rear like a balcony which, they said was a lower platform for passengers to land their water bikes etc., because in no way it is practical to lift such outfits to the deck in the sea. The ship weighs about 1500 tones. The owners of the shipyard Majeed and son Gafoor told me that they are now receiving enquires from South Africa, America and Gulf countries. The ship under construction is for service in Africa.

Kammalis, the group of unskilled manual labourers for raising the heavy planks etc. are another group of workers in the shipyard.

Caulking is done by inserting cottonwicks dipped in oil. Originally it was Marotti or punna oil which is now rare, and groundnut oil or cocoanut oil is used.

People embalming fish oil boiled with lime outside the boat was another group of workers.

A group of carpenters outside the yard used to supply carved and polished parts. Carving and decoration work is done all over such ships as some of the photographs show. Such decorative works would have been there in passenger ships. But medieval times ships were constructed as cargo vessels, which were also used by passengers. Barbossa got four ships constructed in Beypore, because the cost compared to European ships was almost half. A repairing train of crew used to travel in ships as experts. The food on board was mainly rice and vegetables. In the absence of Freezer storage system, meat and fish could not be kept long.

We get a detailed reporte of the first Portuguese ships under Vascoda Gama from the records of Barbossa where, sufficient arrangements were made for the long journey under different climates. To avoid decomposition of victuals on board, living beings that could be used for food were allowed to be transported on board of the ships. Thus fowls, castrated rams, pork, sheep and cocks, were taken into the vessels of Sixteenth century. Cocks were also useful to find out the time based on their morning singings .[4]

The practice might have been adopted in Arab ships too because they were always in need of victuals like mutton, fowls, etc. They could be bought from stores in the ship.

When good catch was made, auction of the fish was conducted. It was also an occasion of entertaimnent on board.

But generally high sea going ships always had a religious atmosphere. Reference has been made earlier for the presence of Sufis, theologians and ulema on board of the Arab ship. A more detailed description of life on board a Portuguese ship, is available in the accounts of Portuguese writers, with a priest appointed by the king and a lot of Jesuit fathers on board travelling to India.

Women were prohibited from travelling on board. The Jesuit fathers conducted a search to see if any were travelling unauthorized and if found, were severely punished because there was a general conviction that the purity of life is essential for successful completion of the voyage. Hence women of bad reputation, if any, were found on board, they were imprisoned and chained.

We have noted the religious discourse for which pious people were carried on board the Arab ship. The affairs were still more religious on European ships.

Holy water was preserved in the vessels. Lent, feast days and processions were observed on board. The oratories and chapels in the vessels were beautifully decorated with panels or framed pictures giving a congenial atmosphere for prayer.

People prayed for all the co-passengers, for the ship and all the things in it. The life of prayer on board a Portuguese ship was quite enviable. The priests on board used to conduct the good news of Christ, singing hymns in honor of blessed Virgin Mary, leading processions and hearing confessions of the people on board. It must be remembered, that faced with a tempest in the sea and prospective disaster, several people went to confession as a preparation for a good death. The sermons were so heart-rending that the people in large numbers went to confusion with deep felt repentance.[5]

The same condition existed in Arab ships too, but the journey from Malabar to Siraf, Basra, Mocha or Ports of Persia were not so long, and climate so different compared to Portuguese Navigation round the Cape of Good hope.

Even vegetables would be damaged in few days. Therefore Rice and Dal, Onion, etc. formed chief items of food in ships owned by natives, mostly constructed in Malabar.

The work of crew was per half day in turn, but even when on leisure they always had to give a helping hand to lower or roll the mast, bail out water and help in the kitchen.

Drinking water was stored in wooden drums made of teak. Only for drinking and cooking, fresh water was used and for all the rest, sea water was used. To meet the shortage rain water was stored.

The passengers did not use Betele for its inconvenience. Selfmade beedies were used. It is reported that even in Portuguese ships, every thing could be bought from the store.

Various rituals and ceremonies were observed in ship-building. Selection of the timber is made in forest fellings 'coop',[6] as they are called. The yard owners or contractors visited the forest, identified the trees which were generally called 'Arabi Size'. Treatise on ship-building propose ***pooja*** of the tree and an auspicious occasion to cut it. But this was not possible in deep interior forests. Here the chief wood cutter would make the first cut. The hours of the day and sunshine etc. are important because the timber cut in the early and very late hours are bound to be easily worm ridden. The days of lunar months are also considered for the same reason. The first 14 days of the lunar month are called '***Ilaravu***' (younger nights) when wood cutting or such things are avoided. Even boiling paddy for keeping long is avoided. Elders said that the grain will be worm or moth eaten.

When the work is completed and ship is ready to be launched the last rite in the yard is performed. The chief Odayi make some marks on either side in ***Aniyam*** (front) of the ship which they believe is the eyes of the ship. The significance is now the ship is born. In the case certain mammals eyes are not clear when a baby is born. With opening of the eye the ship is born, alive and ready to perform its task.

Professor Arunachalam has given details of the eye opening ceremony of ship elsewhere, but not so elaborate in Beypore. Before the boat is let into the water, a major ritual is the 'opening of the eye', cut into the boat-side at the stem end of the prow on both sides by the mater-carpenter accompanied by a mid-night animal sacrifice to ward off evil spirits.[7]

The mast is fixed after launching the ship, when it is in water. This is to avoid inconvenience in handling the ship while launching.

Launching is also done with Prayer by Tangals. The whole beach and visitors gather to lend a helping hand. The Odayis are given substantial rewards now by the owner of the ship, other than the owner of the building yards. A grand feast is arranged and the whole beach gives a festive look.

Launching is done by Khalasis, famous all over the world for their skills. They use a grand wheel and pulleys attached to its rope which go on multiplying in two or three stages before they are connected with the ship. Straight, round mango trees are put on either side of the ship and slowly it is allowed to roll on round woods. The ship is brought near the water on low tide, so that it can be pushed more into the water and when high tide comes with very little effort the ship is moved and the high tidal waves takes in (accepts) the ship. The mast is fixed when the ship is in water.

It is quite likely that more elaborate and intrinsic rituals were conducted during medieval times in the age of patron saints and sea perils. As in the case of Ullal Dargha, where replica of the ship is bestowed as offering, some similar rituals were carried in Beypore too. The Khanqah of the Kazerumi Shaikhs who were patron saints of the sea voyage, existed in Calicut also with such strong in fluence on Mariners where people 'insured' their ship and merchandise in unalterable faith of the Sufi as Spencer Trimmingham puts it. Naturally offerings were sent to such shrines and their blessings were sought.

All the mariners in the emporium of spice trade in Persian Gulf used to assemble in the hospice of Malik Dinar in Basra and offerings should have reached there also. The mariner community in general had profound respect for Malik Dinar and they constructed the earliest ten mosques in trading centres along the Malabar coast.

The origin of the Khalasis' expertise seems to have Persian influence as the name of their chief instrument 'Bavar'[8] for the wheel and 'Naanth'[9] for the ropes (iron) are of Persian origins. The people worked in the bower, with rhythmic tunes of sacred themes.

In some places as noticed in Ponnani songs are composed praising big ships when they are launched. This practice must have existed long before. The Muslims of Malabar coast especially around Beypore have the tradition of composing songs which is called Mala (garland, where each line is strung like pearls in a garland). The songs were earlier composed as hagiographic works but the tradition so influenced the mass that songs were composed on all important events like death of saints, leaders of parties, charisma of Sayyids or even on an accident.

The ships constructed in Beypore were durable and in effective service for comparatively longer period. Barbosa had come across large number of ships in service in the gulf region, constructed in Malabar.

The Odayis reported that ships built in Beypore 60 or 70 years before plying in gulf regions were being brought for repair. These days workshops are established in the gulf regions as well. They import teak from Beypore and other regions. A good number of foreign investors- Arabs, etc. attend the auction of teaks in the government forest yard of Beypore, where only the A1 size teak is stored.[10] Foreign investors. shipyard owners or agents from different ports of the world flock to this auction, rarely held there which used to be regularly held in the past. Teak has many classifications as a standard timber.

'L.L(long length) was the size of teak which was in great demand for urus. This size is not available now even in government plantations. The next in quality are graded as follows:[11]

A. 7-10 mtrs length: 150-185 cms.
   Where the girth is uniform throughout its length. This is called 1st class and super quality.

B1. 7-10 mtrs length: 150-185 cms girth with bends and twists.

B2. 7-10 mtrs length: Lesser girth which is generally used for house construction etc.

B3. 7-10 mtrs length: Lesser girth used for furniture and other body works and frames.
Poles : ·Slender teak, generally sold after selection felling in plantation. Useful in furniture and works.

The teak is cut and stored from the government plantations in Nilambur, started by the British government in 1845.

The collector of Malabar H.V. Conolly, started the teak plantation in Nilambur for the British government. This was intended to make sufficient teak available for the Bombay ship-building yard and for Railways. For convenient transportation of teak, a Railway line was constructed from Shornur to Nilambur, terminating in a nearby place called Mukkatta. The project was a great success. By 1900 Bombay shipyard rivalled any other of its kind in the world. Conolly's plot where a few of the oldest teak trees are still preserved, is a tourist spot. In recognition of the importance of Nilambur teak, the state government has established a 'Teak Museum' in Nilambur where a visitor can get good idea of history, size and science of teak.

Valapattanam (Badfatan of Arabs) was another centre of ship-building. When the strike of 1980s, which lasted for 10 years, paralysed the shipbuilding activities, Odayis migrated to other centres while unskilled labourers like Kammalis and even skilled labourers like Khalasis lost their jobs. Distant centres like Valapatanam and Mangalore were selected by investors and sponsors. But in Valapatanam, there were not many takers for shipbuilding, though it was a centre, noted by foreign travellers like Varthema and Barbosa, was not very impressive. One of the reason for the cold response may be the non-proximity of feeder forests.

The Sulka shipyard here recently constructed a pleasure boat of Sambook, type on orders from Qatar. Its Keel was 60 ft, completed in 2009. The ship was constructed for Shaikh Abdulla bin Fahad Althani of the Qatar Royal family within 2 years, and tugged to Dubai, where the interior decorations were completed. It had many Royal suites. Dining hall, coffee bar and decks for sunbath. Hashim the owner of the Sulka shipyard, was kind enough to give me some of the photographs of the ship after the decoration works in Dubai.

Reference

1. B. Arunachalam, ***Indian Tradition of Boat-building in Pius Malekandathil*** and Jamal Muhammed (Ed), ***The Portuguese, Indian Ocean and European, Bridge Heads 1500-1800***, p. 35.
2. The biggest ship ever built in Beypore is now under construction in Binafa Enterprise yard/at Beypore with 145 ft keel.
3. The ribs have to be sturdy and load bearing. Rib timber is never straight. It is of V shape of sharply angular. In most vessels rib logs are crude, retaining their original rough form. Timber for ribs is preferred in their natural state of grain and curvature; many shorts to medium sized tropical hardwoods provide such timber cheap (B. Arunachalam, ***op.cit.***, p. 382)
4. K.S, Mathew, ***Life on board a Portuguese Ship during the Sixteenth Century. Studies in History of Deccan Medieval and Modern*** (Ed.). M.A. Nayeem, etc. p. 176.
5. ***Ibid.***, p. 174.
6. Division of forest, marked for felling trees and auctioned to bidders.
7. Arunachalam, ***op.cit.***, p. 385-6.
8. The wooden wheel the major equipment of Khalasis to lift the vehicles or launch the ships etc.
9. The Persian word for rope as the Khalasis use.
10. The teak is then sawed and carried to the gulf yards and building yards in other countries. Teak has many specification in markets. There was a size 'L.L.' 'Long Length', as it was called. It is a 7-10 meter timber with above 100 to 150 ems girth, a log, and of uniform girth right though its length.
11. Interview with Timber merchants who regularly send truckloads of Timber to various building yards and goes round to collect money on every Saturdays and Sundays. It was a matter of astonishment that one of the leading suppliers did not need any account book reference for his collections of money.

CHAPTER-VII

Social Impact of Maritime Activities

Various occupational groups at different levels were associated with maritime activities in trading centres.

Abdurazzak, The Persian Ambassador has given a detailed description of the city and market place of Calicut, which was almost the same all over the Malabar Coast except in the case of treatment wrecked ships.

Arab travellers, grouped as Arab geographers have noted the land, cities, people, fauna and flora of Malabar. Some of them were reports[1] from travellers and therefore near truth or exaggerated or mistaken in transcription. For example, when describing pepper, it is reported that pepper bunches grow under each leaf and when it rains the leaf comes down to protect the bunch.

All cultivated and forest produces of spice are recorded. These spices which brought gold to 'market places' also brought social and cultural influences in trade intercourse. This trade required sufficient ocean-going ships, locally constructed. Big traders who had business transactions and ware houses in different parts of the world, possessed number of vessels.

Nakhuda Misqal with whom Ibn Batuta travelled from Ormuz to Calicut was a big merchant who had many ships plying between Jawa, etc. and gulf. He constructed the famous 'Misqal Palli' Misqual Masjid which stands even now as a unique structure intact in the Muslim Centre of Calicut, used for five time prayers and Friday congregations.

The Egyptian, Karimi merchants were very rich and carried almost all the business of Calicut. People of other nationalities like Persians, Arabs, Turks, Africans, Chinese, Tunisians, Sinhalese, of other nations and Indians like Bohras and Seths of Gujarat, the Naiks of Konkan Chettis of Eastern Coast, all had warehouses in Calicut.

In other words there had been investors from all over the then civilized world. This process gave rise to unimaginable changes. The investors required helpers, Brokers-agents and servants. Abdurazzack, the Ambassador from the Sultan of Heerat, though not very happy on his arrival in Calicut speaks of the facilities provided for foreigners. The Zamorin had assigned him a house, a clerk, a servant and provisions of flour, ghee, sugar, fowls, etc. Thus large number of skilled and unskilled people came in contact with foreigners. On the arrival of a ship in a port, the traders had to make arrangements for carts to carry the merchandize to market places. Naturally sailors collected fresh water from suppliers, and also daily provisions like milk, oil, vegetables, fish and meat. A good number of people were also required as carriers in markets because in Calicut like other cities of Malabar animals as carriers of burden were not in use, but loads were carried overhead. This has been referred elsewhere in the work as interestingly noted by Ibn-Batuta.[2]

The native people could naturally contrast their own conditions with the foreigners. Hence Abdurazzack's observations are more relevant. When he landed in Calicut, the natives resembled to him devils who were all black and naked, having only a piece of cloth tied round their middle, and holding in one hand a shining javelin, and in the other a buckler of bullock's hide. He met the King in a 'similar state of nudity' though the hall was adorned with paintings and flanked by two or three thousand attendants. This mode of dress of the ruler of Calicut and his attendants has well been described by all the foreigners. The same dress of a piece of cloth hanging from the waist upto to the knee while the whole body was smeared with sacred ashes and with anklets of gold and diamond was noted when Vasco Da Gama paid his obeisance to Zamorin. While the foreigners, especially the Arabs and Persians dressed in most elegant manner riding on fine horses[3] and residing in magnificent houses.

This inequality in all aspects of life was naturally a temptation for change. The life style is adopted every where without changing religion and beliefs; always a superior life style is just adopted and accepted. Those who were engaged in services of traders and in market places were not people of high caste, Brahmins or Nairs. They were mainly Ezhavas who were more concentrated in palms and coastal areas where coconut palms grow in abundance, because these were more coconut pluckers and toddy tappers. The first native converts might have come from this community. One of my conviction for this proposition is as follows. For any work connected with coconut palm either coconut plucking or toddy tapping, a very sharp knife is necessary, so that an Ezhava is always seen with a sharp knife in a scabbard hung on his waistband. Muslims till recently were always dressed with a lungi belt and a sharp knife hung from it as part of his attire. This knife was much dreaded by British officials in Malabar as 'war knives' which were confiscated in 1840s. It was a measure to prevent 'Mappila outrages' as the Britishers called the peasant outrages of 18th century. This general acceptance of war knifes is seen only among Mappilas, and in no other communities.

The introduction of Zoroastrianism, Judaism, Christianity and Islam to Malabar was also the work of Maritime traders.

No need to attempt to trace ancient history in this context. Arabs had trade and navigation monopoly in eastern trade. When the Abbasid Caliphs were ruling in Baghdad and the whole of Arabia, Egypt, Persia, Central Asia to the boundaries of India, north Africa and on the European continent, the present Spain and part of Portugal were under their banners. Four hundred years of Pax-Islamica (Islamic peace) brought prosperity to Caliphal empire arts of peace, learning and science developed. The net result was the emergence of a flourishing bureaucracy, a vast consuming class throughout the empire. This increase of consuming class further improved the scope and profit of traders of eastern luxuries.

This was the time when Muslims had no rivals on land or sea.

The immense profit of spice trade was one of the causes for the European attempts led by Portuguese to find out a sea route round the Cape to India.[4]

In Maritime centres, there was sufficient scope for spread of Islam. Arab Muslims had settlement colonies in all trading centres all over the world, so much so that once in 9th century Caliph's subjects were able to sack and burn 1/3rd of the town Kanfu over a conflict.

A medieval ship had always an air of spirituality, be it a trading vessel or passenger ship. There was the practice of ships plying with pilgrims to Mecca either as groups or sponsored by a Prince (as in the case of Mughal princes, princesses and nobles). Sometimes they purchased ships for such specific purposes or leased for trade. The ship- owner Nakhuda, more often stayed in the ship and captained the ship or employed another captain to lead the ship. The ***Hajj*** Pilgrims were always pious people.

There was a strange practice of Mariners carrying holymen on board for various purposes. Sometimes the pious men out of zeal, to propagate Islam opted to travel farthest corners they may reach and became passengers in trading ships to preach Islamic faith. The ship-owners encouraged such men as passengers since they were useful on various occasions. As Professor Athar Abbas Rizvi has pointed, Mariners and traders encouraged adventurous preachers and Mystics to accompany them for various reasons.[5] Firstly, to give them spiritual training engaging their leisure hours. Secondly, they would provide the mariners spiritual solace and composure in the face of hair-raising calamities on the sea. Thirdly, they believed that their presence would protect the ship and crew from dangers and fourthly, these pious people acted as mediators between them and natives of the lands where ever they may touch, in case of any dispute or bargain. Ibn Batuta has mentioned such practices among fishermen[6] and sailors.

Many of the Sayyids, Sufis and holymen on board later settled in the port of destination. In every trading centres there had been ***Jaram*** (Qabar) of such people whom people venerated as saints.

Sufi Khanqahs of various Sufi Silsilas actively functioned and flourished in all trading centres of Eastern seas. The best testimony is

'Rehla'. By virtue of being introduced to any Sufi order in any part of the world, a person could avail hospitality in the Khanqah of that Sufi order anywhere in the world.

Many of the Sufis were patron saints of Mariners. Often different trade guilds had separate patron saints. The trade guilds and their patron saints of Mariners in each seas were so powerful that it was under the banner of guilds they went in groups to '*Idgaha*'[7] in some places in Muslim countries. The Khanqa served as hospices for traders in important cities, where members of particular Sufi orders could retire after their day's business, listen to discourses of pious men, participate in common rituals and recite individual '***Dhikr*** and ***Dua***'[8]. Spencer Trimmingham called these Khanquah as 'Pious night clubs'.

Khanqahs were an intgral part of maritime life in medieval world. Not spiritual or religious, but of great economic significance. During the voyage in the face of any disaster or peril, the captain would vow to pay an amount to the Khanqah of patron saint if the calamity is averted and his ship reaches safely its destination. He would write down the amount in a bill. This will be repeated many times and the captain would write down his vows. By the time the ship reaches its port of destination a sufficiently good amount will be vowed, when the ship is anchored in the port, the agents from the Khanqah would approach the captain and receive the amount vowed to their Khanqah.

In this way every ship approaching a trade centre was sure to have vowed cash, so much so that the Khanqah custodians even sent their credit bills to ships to clear it from the vowed amount, Spencer Trimmingham calls this custom a "Powerful insurance system".[9] They ensured their security by such vows. In all the eastern seas Kazeruni Sufis were patron saints of Mariners. Khuzeruni Khanquahs flourished in Malabar in Calicut, Quilon and Kasaragode and as far as coasts of Bengal and Trade centres in Assam as Ibn Batuta have us believe. He had availed the hospitality in Kazeruni Khanqahas in all these places.

For better convenience, traders and travellers got initiated to more than one Tariqua. lbn-Batuta himself had resorted to this practice.

These Khanqahs with their immense resources and the pious and holy existence of the Sufis contributed greatly to the spread of Islam in

Malabar. The Muslim traders made sufficient contributions as charity, poor sight and Hadiya.[10] During his stay in Quilandy (North Quilon) Ibn-Batuta visited the Juma Masjid where he saw 300 students undergoing religious education. They were staying in the Masjid, fed from common kitchen where "the expenditure was met from the contribution of shipowners visiting the port".

All important ports on Malabar coast had shrines of Patron saints to whom devotees went on ascribing miracles. Even every village of fishermen on coast had patron saints who 'blessed them with good catch, protected them on seas, safeguarded their settlements from rough sea' and erosion which is common in all rainy season. It were they who protected them from disease as the people believed.

The Dargha of Hazrath Madani in Ullal, near Kasaragode is best example. The present writer noted bags of cardamom and large number of replica of ships. I was told that these were offered to the Dargha for fulfilling vows made on calamities on sea. The crew would make a vow to offer a measure of cardamom, some money and a replica of the ship. Cardamom as an offering is surely the continuation of old practice. Annual Urs is conducted in the Dargha of Ullal. Fisher folk and ship- owners all consider it auspicious to participate in the Urs. The main feature is religious discourses and prayers, but the most important event is the feast which continues for many days. Mariners and common people all over Malabar maintain such belief in his ***Karama*** (Miracle) that anybody can offer a goat for the feast anywhere. They fasten a small bag in its neck, devotees offer fruits, etc. to the goat and deposit coins in the bag. Nobody dares to harm the goat even if it destroys crops or eat vegetable and fruits. Everybody very cautiously guided the goat in the direction of ***Ullal.*** Finally devotees believe that by the ***Karama*** of the saint, many number of such goats would arrive in the Dargh during the days of feast. The devotees even pronounce only very polite and respectable words while referring to such sacrificial goats. All riverine settlements too have patron saints, their raised tombs or a tomb attached to the Juma Masjid.

Sufism thus played a very important role in the overall activities of economic life in medieval times especially in the communities of

Mariners. Mass conversion of functional groups[11] like Marakkars also took places and Islam spread far and wide.

There was another envious phenomena of the migration of Sayyids of Hadramawt from seventeenth century onwards. These people known as Sayyids of Hadramawt, were descended from the tribe of Prophet Mohammed and were held in High esteem all over the world. Large scale migration of Hadrami Sayyids to all over the eastern ports especially Malabar cannot be attributed to any specific cause, but it is believed that the Portuguese presence in the Persian gulf had an adverse effect on their social status, income and prestige. These people were held in high reverence and on their landing, the rulers recognized them as leaders of communities, granting annual income and marks of honour as we see in the case of Mamburam Tangal (The Sayyid of Mamburam), who was recognized as the head of Mappilas by the Zamorin and on the succession ceremony, the robe of honour was sent by the king.

The intermingling of Hindus and Muslims were so close that even Hindu folk deities were given the names of Muslims.

Theyyam of Alichamundi was one of the examples. Chamundi was a beautiful folk goddess. She was taking bath in a pond. Ali who passed by, was so attracted by the beauty of Chamundi who did not know that she was goddess. He went near her and began to disturb her. The goddess out of anger cursed him to death. But the devotees thought since Ali was killed by Chamundi they must diefy him with the name 'Alichamundi'.

In all Theyyam and Thiras of north Malabar, the head dress resembles a mast, indeed a very tall mast, quite different from the head dress of traditional art form like 'Kathakali' or 'Ottamthullal'. So is the tradition of 'Ali Bappan Theyyam'.

The rise and growth of merchant princes like Zamorin of Calicut was mainly the work of maritime traders. The Zamorins territory was a marshy plain on the seashore. By conferring favours and patronage on maritime traders, he gained the richness and prosperity of his kingdom. Calicut as safest harbour on Malabar coast was famous. But this safety was characteristic of the entire medieval trade custom. Ibn Jubair the

Spanish Hajj pilgrim of fourteenth century, starting from Granda through Alexandria preferred a parallel route to Nile to cross red sea near the location of present Jeddah. He described the savage wild almost naked tribes of present Sudan who would attack and rob passengers. At the same time he saw pepper bags heaped like sand bags on the wayside. They were property of traders who were compelled to leave them probably due to the death of carrying camel. But no one would touch it except its owner when he comes back. Such a tradition had been in existence in Arab trade. By the hospitality and favour extended to Muslims, Zamorin was known in the west as a 'Moorish prince'.

The Zamorins adopted a splendid tradition in the case of wrecked ships. In all other ports, if a ship bound for some other port was driven by calamities to a port other than its port of destination, people would plunder it saying that God has given them the ship. But in Calicut harbour no harm was done to any ships bound to any port. Calicut was the greatest emporium of spice trade. In the words of Pyrard de Laval, "This merchant prince attracted the whole wealth of the globe to his market place". Shayah Zainuddin the author of Tuhfat ul ***Mujahideen***, noted in 1573 that expansion of empire and urbanization of the kingdom was the work of Arabs. "The increase in the number of cities was due to them" (Muslims).

The twelfth century Sanskrit work '***Musaka Vamsamkavya***' of Atula on the Musakavamsa dynasty of Ezhimala[12] has also reference that after founding his capital 'Nakulan brought men from far off Islands and settled them in his capital' obviously traders at the flourishing days of Arab Muslim trade.

Tipu Sultan had well understood the significance of a trade outlet on the west coast, and planned to establish his capital in a very strategic land on the Chaliyar confluence which he named Farooqabad now called Feroke, the plan did not any way materialize.[13]

The spread of Shafi sect on Malabar was an importent feature of Muslims population of the area. Once this question was asked to the great scholar late Pr fessor K.A. Nizami, Why, when all over India Hanafi sect is in majority, how it happened in Malabar alone, Shafi sect spread? The answer was: Because it is the Shafi school which has discussed the rules of trade threadbare. Since the origin of the community was mainly from traders, Shafi sect was accepted.[14]

The best example of mutual influence of communities is Sabarimala, the biggest shrine of Hindu congregation in south India. The tradition is that Sri Ayyappa, the diety, had a close friend 'Vavar' whose origin is also associated with sea and ships. They were so close that while Ayyappa was deified, a shrine was also erected for his close friend nearby where a Masjid was constructed. The devotees performing pilgrimage should first bestow their offerings to Vavar at the Masjid and then proceed to the chief deity Ayyappa. Vavar has become an ***Upaprathishta.***

Another case is that of Othenan and Kujali Marakkar. Othenan, one of the hero of Northern Ballads (Vadakkan Pattukal) was a very close friend of Kunjali Maraldmr, the Naval captain of Zamorins of Calicut. Their enemies had always conspired against them, without success. Both were defeated when they parted ways due to many compulsions.

Social Impact

The close association of Muslim mariner traders with the rulers of Calicut is revealed in ***Mamankam. Mamankam*** was a great assembly met in the lunar month of Magha, once in twelve years following the Jupiter (***Brihaspati***) cycle. Thirunavaye was one of the many centres where such twelve-yearly river festivals were conducted in ancient India, like Kumbhakonam, Gokarnam, Nasik, Ujjayini, Haridwar, Prayag etc. In post-Cera period in Kerala, this place came under the Raja of Valluvanad and by virtue of this position, he was to preside over the grand festival as the ***Rakshapurusha*** (Protector).

In the period of expansion of Kozhikode kingdom during 13th and 14th centuries, the Zamorin of Calicut was looking for new adventures. The chieftains of the Thirumanasseri Nadu appealed to Zamorin to protect him from the attack of Valluvanad. This gave the Zamorin an excuse to move into the territory of Valluvanad. The Kozhikode Army of Nayars advanced by land and the Kozhikkottu Koya proceeded with four ships along the river. According to Calicut

Grandhavari, the Zamorin was able to capture Valluvanad and thereby appropriated the status of ***Rakshapurusha*** for the festival.

It is stated in this ***Grandavari*** that the Zamorin rewarded the Koya who had instigated the attack and supported him, by permitting the later to stand on his right side[15] on the grand platform known as 'Nilapadutara' at Vakayur on the occasion of the festival. He was given the title of Shah Bantra Koya, chief officer-in-charge of the port of Kozhikode. He enjoyed all privileges and dignities of a Nayar Chief, Jurisdiction over all the Mohammedans residing in the Bazar, the right to receive small presents from the Ezhavas, the Kammalas and the Mukkuvas whenever the Zamorin conferred any honours on them[16] on ceremonial occasions.

It seems that the official historian of the Zamorins, is mistaken that the title of Shah Bandar was conferred as a reward for the help on capturing of Tirunavaya, because from 10th century onwards we hear of Shahbandar (Commissioner of Port) in 'Eastern Seas' and Calicut, the emporium of spice trade probably had "Shah Bandar Khwaja' earlier, who was head of Muslims of Calicut. One family still exists in Calicut as the house of 'Sabantra Koya'. [17] Kazi Mohammed in his ode ***Fathhul Mubim*** calls him as "Raeesul Muslimeen" (Head of Muslims). With many other honours he was also authorized to pull down the roofs of criminals as a punishment for serious offences.

With the growing power and prosperity of the Zamorin, the ***Maha Magha*** festival at Tirunavaye assumed all Kerala significance. The rulers and chieftains of the land who came under the Zamorin used to send tribute and flags of fealty on receiving the official invitation to attend the Mamankam. It was an occasion for pilgrims, traders, scholars and all sorts of people to congregate there.

In short Muslim mariners and traders had a great role in making the kingdom of Calicut prosperous and upholding its glory and grandeur. This was one of the examples of 'Cultural Symbiosis'[18] as professor M.G.S. Narayanan rightly recorded.

Maritime impacts on ·society at various levels are identical only of this earliest Muslim community of south -east Asia, while such an impact is absent in society elsewhere in India.

Reference

1. Ibn Khurdadbeh, one of the important Arab geographers was Post Master General of Siraf. The head of the Postal department was designated as Sahibul Barid wal Akbar (Head of Post and Intelligence) who had all facility for collecting information from traders, travelers, intelligence and travel accounts.
2. There were no horse or beasts of bmihen, and that everything had to be carried on men's backs, who hired themselves for this purpose.
3. Matters were just reversed when the Portuguese arrived, usurped high sea trade and monopolized spice trade. When Shaikh Zainuddin compiled ***Tuhfat*** in 1573 one of his complaint was that 'They (The Portuguese) make Muslims run in front of their horses. (***Tuhfat....***)
4. C.R. Boxer, ***The Portuguese Seaborne Empire (1415-1825)***, London (1969), pp· 17 ff. "The main impulses behind the 'Age of Discovery' evidently came from a mixture of religions, economic, strategic and political factors".
5. Athar Abbas Rizvi, ***Sufism in India***, Appendix on Sufi's of Deccan and South India.
6. Taking pious holy men on board was believed to bring good luck. P.R.G. Mathur has noted that Mappila fishermen of Tamn· sometimes took a Sayyid or Musliar with them for a good catch on fishing expedition.
7. Place of congregation on the days of ld and Bakrid of Muslims.
8. Prayers.
9. Spencer Trimmingham. ***Sufiordus in Islam***, pp. 9-12.
10. Hadiya, Voluntary gift given by a man.
11. Mass conversion of functional groups especially in vocation like trade etc. were not common. Mass conversion of Parava community of pearl fishery of east coast to Christianity during Portuguese period.
12. The site of present Naval Academy of Ezhimala.
13. On the hill on the left bank of Chaliyar, some underground entrance from a well leads to a hall with arched roof. People say that it was a secret passage opening some where in to the river. The ASI has marked the site as a protected monument.
14. The Muslims all over the world have adopted one of the four theological set in Islam, Shaft, Hanaft Maliki and Hambali originated from all the four great scholars. All along Malabar Shaft sect is popular while in the rest of the country other sects mainly Hanaft are popular, with minor variations in observations.
15. Qazi Muhammad, ***Fathhul Mubin*** (1573)
16. K.V. Krishna Ayyar, ***The Zamorins of Calicut***, pp. 99-100.
17. My friend late Dr. S.M. Mohammad Koya had introduced me to a member of the house Sabantra Koya, one of his neighbours in the oldest Muslim residence centre of Kuttichira in Calicut.
18. M.G.S. Narayanan, ***Cultural Symbiosis in Kerala***. Kerala Historical Society, Trivandrum (1972).

Bibliography

Primary Sources

Abulfazal, ***Akbarnama***

Aminumantakath Pareekutty Musliyar, Muhimmathul Muminin (Ar. Manuscript 1921)

Buchanan Francis, H., ***A Journey Through Mysore, Canara and Madras,*** 3 vols. London (1807)

Kunhayin Musliar, Kappappattu, Ca 1500.

Logan William, ***Malabar District Manual,*** Madras (1887).

M.L. Dames, ***The Book of Durate Barbosa,*** Hakluyt Society Second Series, Vol. II, (1921).

N.M. Naboothiri, ***Calicut Grandhavari*** (Palm Leaf Manuscript (Mal.), dated, 1667 AD)

Qadi Muhammad, ***Fathhul Mubin,*** (Ar) 1573.

Sheikh Zainuddin Makhdum (Senior), ***Hidayat ul Adhkiya Ila Tariqat il Auliya*** (Ar- 1540)

______, ***Tuhfatul Mujahidin Fi Baazi Ahwal al Burthuqaliyyin*** (1573).

Author uncertain (Ca 1520), ***Adbhutha Ratna Mala*** or ***Kottuppalli Mala*** (Arabi-Malayalam) Many times reprinted by devotees).

F. Steingass, ***Persian English Dictionary,*** Delhi (1973).

Athar Abbas Rizvi, ***A History of Sufism in India,*** Delhi (1999).

Ahmnmad Moulavi, C.N. & K.K. Muhammad Abdul Karim, Mahathaya Mappila Sahithya Parambaryam.

Anirudha Ray, M.A. Nayeem and K.S. Mathew (ed), ***Studies in History of Deccan, Medieval and Modern.***

Arun Kumar Misra, Trading Communities in Ancient India. From Earliest Times to 300AD. Delhi (1992).

Boxer, C.R. Joao de Barros..

Danvers, F.C., ***The Portuguese in India,*** London (1894).

Dasgupta, A., ***Malabar in Asian Trade, 1740-1840,*** Cambridge (1967).

Disney, A.R., ***Twilight of the Pepper Empire,*** Harward (1978).

El-Khazraji, ***History of Rasuli Dynasty,*** London (1906-1918).

Ganesh, K.N. (ed.), ***Exercises in Modern Kerala History,*** Kottaymn (2012).

Gibb, H.A.R., ***Travels in Asia and Africa, 1325-1354,*** New York (1929).

Goitein, S.D., ***Studies in Islamic History and Institutions,*** Leyden (1966).

Greenley, W.B., ***The Voayages of Pedro ALvares Cabral to Brazil and India.***

Hadi Hassan, ***History of Persian Navigation.***

Hourari Geroge Fadlo, ***Arab Seafaring in the Indian Ocean in Ancient and Early Medieval Times.*** Princeton (1951).

Ibn Meeran Kutty, ***Mamburam Sayyid Alavi Tangal*** (Mal.), Tirurangadi (1967).

Ittaman, ***Amini Islands.***

Krishna Aiyar, K.V., ***The Zamorins of Calicut,*** Calicut (1938)

Kurup, K.K.N and Mathew, K.M. (Ed.), ***Portuguese Trade with India in the Sixteenth Century,*** Calicut (2000).

Kurup, K.K.N. (Ed), ***India's Naval Traditions,*** New Delhi (1997) Mammad Koya Parappil, ***Kozhikotte Muslimkalude Charithram*** (Mal).

Mathew, K.S., ***Mariners, Merchants and Oceans: Studies in Maritime History,*** New Delhi (1995).

______, ***Ship-building and Navigation in the Indian Ocean Region AD 1400- 1800,*** New Delhi.

Mathur, P.R.G., The Mappila Fisher Folk of Kerala, Trivandrum

(1978). Miller, R.E., ***Mappila Muslims of Kerala***, Madras (1976).

Muhammed Kunhi, P.K., ***Muslimkalum Kerala Charithravum*** (Mal.), Trichur (1980).

Nainar S.M.H., ***Arab Geographers Knowledge of South India***, Madras (1942).

Namboothiri, N.M., ***Kozhikotte Sthala Namangal*** (Mal.), Narayanan, M.G.S., Cultural Symbiosis. Trivandrum (1972)

______, ***City of Truth Revisited***, Calicut (2008).

______, ***Perumals of Kerala***, Calicut (1996).

Panikkar, K.M., ***A History Kerala, 1498-1801***, Annamalai Nagar (1990).

Pius Malekandathil and Jamal Mohammed (Ed.), ***The Portuguese, Indian Ocean and European Bridge Heads- 1500-1800***

Qadiri Shamshullah, ***Malaibar***, Tellichery (2001).

Qaisar, A.J., ***Indian Response to European Technology and Culture***, Delhi (1982).

Raja, P.K.S., ***Medieval Kerala***, Annamalai (1953).

Spencer, Tirimmingham, ***Sufi Orders in Islam.*** Oxford (1971).

Sulaiman Nadvi Sayyid, ***Arabon Ki Jehazarani*** (Trans. Mal), Arabikalude Kappal0:ottam. K.K.M.A. Karim Tirurkad (1976).

Tapan Ray Chaudhari and Irfan Habib, ***Cambridge Economic History of India.***

Teutonio R D'Souza (Ed.), ***Essays on Goan History.***

Thurston, E., ***Castes and Tribes of South India***, Vol. IV, Reprint. Madras (1967).

Tim Severin, ***The Sindbad Voyage.***

Articles

Serjeant, R.B., ***Materials for South Arabian History***, BSOAS, XIII (1), (1949).

Mohammed Koya, S.M., ***Mutta Marriage among the Muslims of Malabar***, IHC, Hyderabad Session (1978).

Fawcett, "War Songs of the Mappilas of Malabar", Indian Antiquar:v, XXX(1901).

Abdurahiman, K.V., ***Ponnani: A Brief Historical Account***, M.E.S. Ponnani, College Souvenir (1969).

Appendices

APPENDIX - I

The light representing a sacred day 'Baraat'

The flags all in tune with mariners system representing various ceremonies (Illegible)

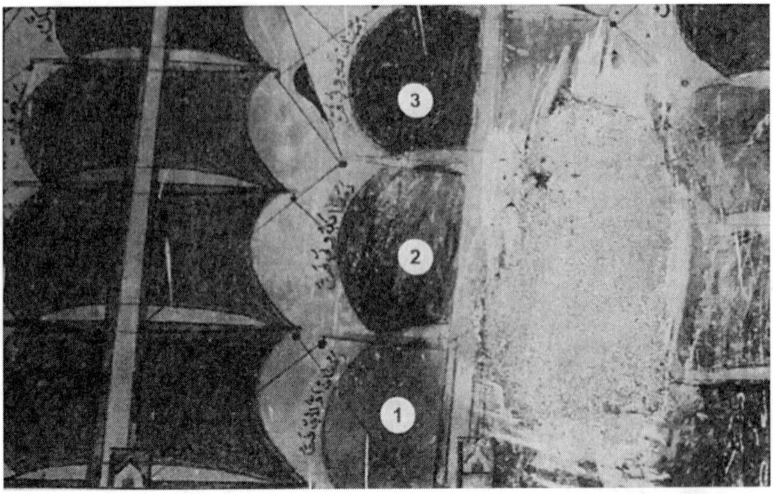

The mast of fast in ascending order is given the 1st ten, IInd ten, IIrd ten

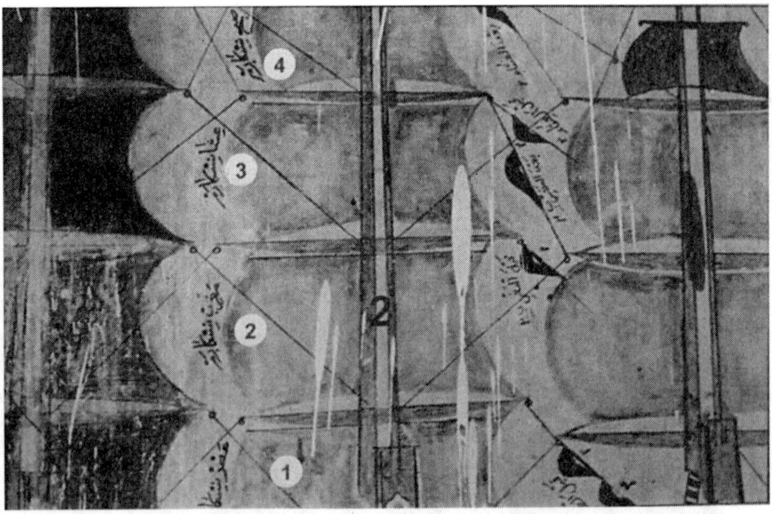

2 Mast second. Bottom not seen. 1. Evening prayer,
2. Prayer at sunset 3. Prayer at night and 4. Prayer before sunrise

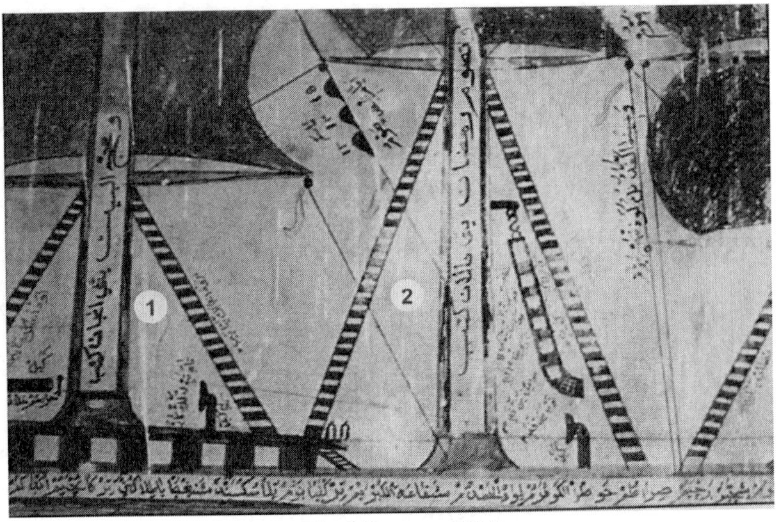

1. The fifth mast of Hajj

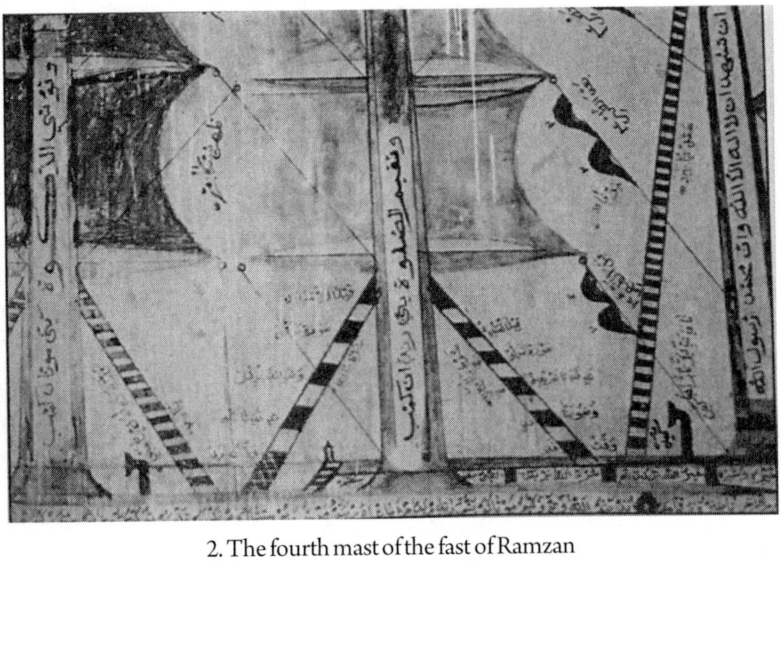

2. The fourth mast of the fast of Ramzan

Sukkan of Aqil. Rudder of Wisdom

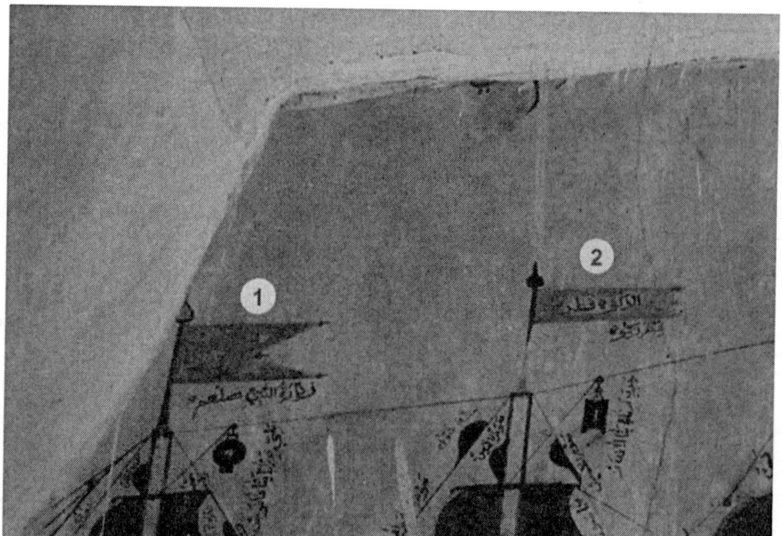

1. On the fifth Mast Hajj, the flag of Ziyarathunnabi
2. On the fourth Mast poor right, the flag of Zakatul Jithr (The Ramzan Zakath)

The Arabi Malayalam Writings at the Bottom of the Painting

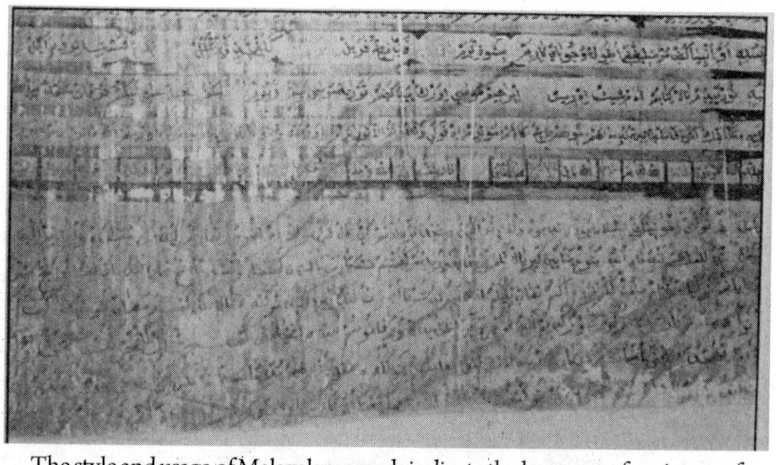

The style and usage of Malayalam words indicate the language of a mixture of Tamil and Malayalam before Malayalam developing separate language

The poem to decide the time of prayers during day measuring ones own shadow

Arabic calligraphy. The same sentences written from right and left

Engraved decorative Amaram (rear) of a ship

The Amaram of a ship built in Beypore in the Background of Dubai

Decorated interior of the Uru built in Valapattanam

Aniyam (front) end of keel with Thathila supporting front and adding grandeur to the ship

Interior of an Uru after completion

Interior of the ship builtin Valapattanam decorated in the gulf

A Ship decorated for launching see the eyes marked.

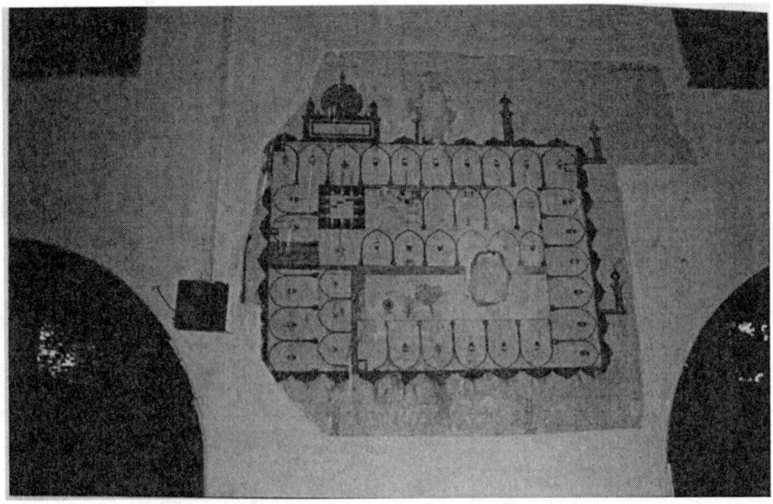

A drawing of Kaaba and Surroundings on the visit of aut/Jor

Imitation of the drawing after the introduction of steam ship- incomplete

The rear end of the Keel

'Korwan' the arch shaped rear end. The space to Ox the fans of the engine

The vari (Ribs) fixed to the keel

Framework of the interior of the largest ship to be decorated in the gulf regions

The raw 'V' shape vari fixed to keel

Planks fixed to varis

The Keel 145ft long 16'x 18'

Side view of the ship under construction

Fixing the iron nails slowly in the holes bored with drills

The special deck which may come in water level to station water bikes

APPENDIX-II

A Direct and Sometimes Literal Translation of the Relevant Lines of Kappapattu (Song of Ship)

All those who live in memory of God
    Think and remember good and see (live)
When vice thoughts are ridden off
    (And then you) Left laziness (to do good) and work enthusiastically
(But) IF (one goes) after lust and ill will
The whole life will be stained black (spoiled)
We have a beautiful ship
    Measuring nine 'chan' in length
The centre if you measure
    With a thread held straight
Full. 'Pandikkooru' length fifty one
    And fixed to Tahathila (bottom plank)
Good ribs (vari) eight on eight side
    An the planks fixed in them
There are seven nails on them
    In the mountain (ship/human body) (is) a store
One 'chan' each in depth
    It has nine doors opening out
Most important three (of them) doors
    Planks 8 x 9 pieces
In the ship done (constructed) by Subbuh (God)
    The most important commodity is heart
Hundred and.twenty-one joints
    444 curves of the body 70000 veins
If all these organs function well (in good manner) the ship moves

safely to its port of destination–God/paradise-

Note: This first four lines are advise common. 'Chan', the length is not clear especially 'Pandichan' (A measurement of length in use in Tamil Country earlier). The vari or ribs eight on either side is the real human ribs.

The human body is a store where the most important commodity loaded in is human heart. Then there is number of joints, carves and veins which should all perform well for the pleasant journey (life) to the port of destination–god.

The language is a mixture Arabic, Persian, Tamil, Telugu and Jasari. Jasari is the language in use in Lacadives in those days. "Jasari' takes it origin from Jaseera-Island–a mixture of the languages of all those who touched and passed through the Island. Lacadives were a place to collect fresh water for Mariners.